100 AMA
ABOUT THE NEG

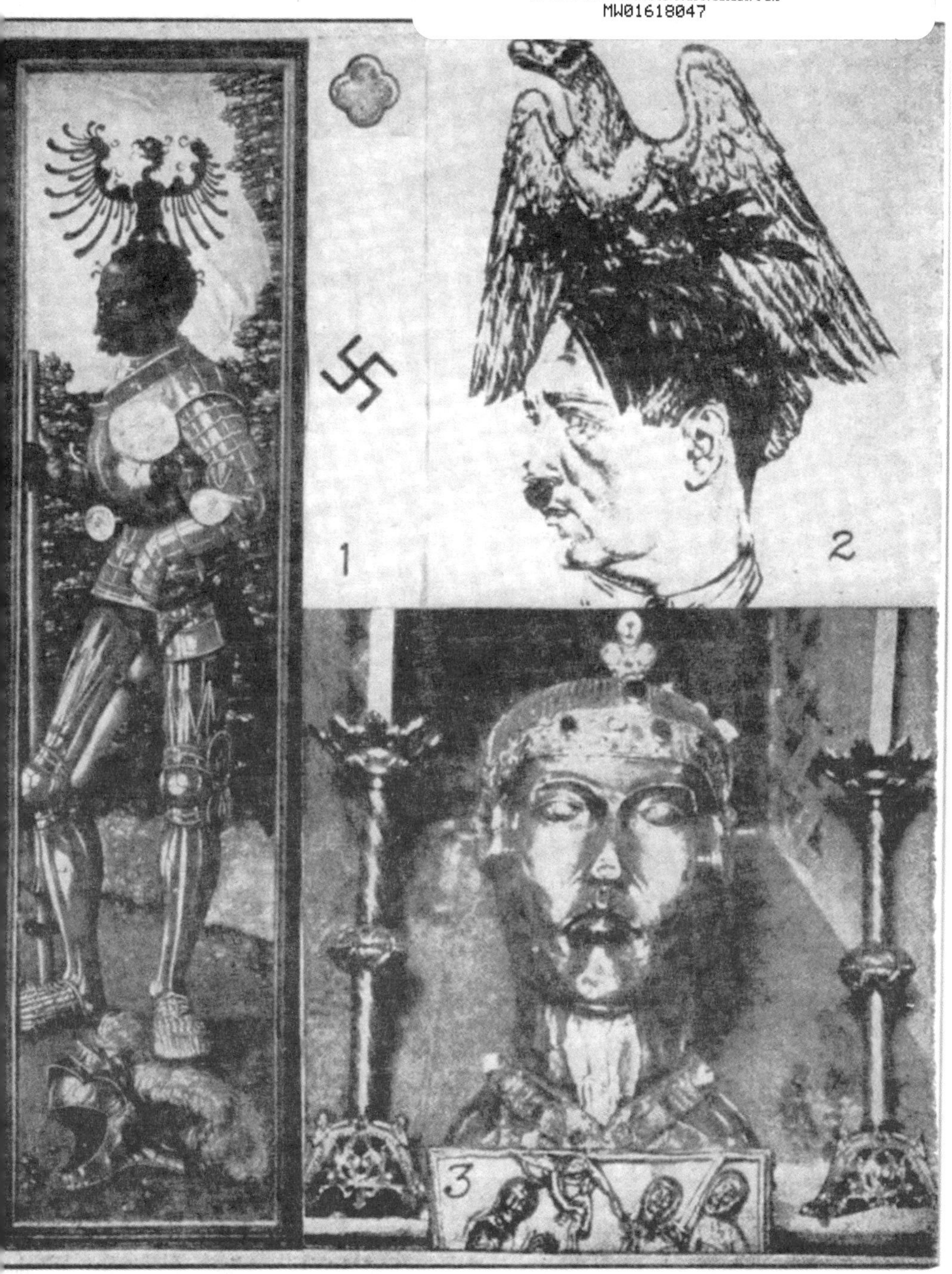

A BLACK CHAMPION OF GERMANY AND A WHITE ONE

(See Proof No. 53)

1. St. Maurice, celestial saint of Germany, wearing the German eagle on his head. 2. Hitler, turies later, also with the German eagle. 3. Golden jeweled mask of St. Maurice in the treasure the Abbey of St. Maurice in Switzerland. Note the Negroid aspect of the mask.

GEN ALFRED A. DODDS

(For biographical data see section 82, page 38 in this book)

"THE BRAVEST OF THE BRAVE"

SOME CONGRESSIONAL MEDAL AND VICTORIA CROSS WINNERS.

(See Proof No. 85)

ANCIENT NEGRO GODS OF THE OLD AND NEW WORLD

1. The Sphinx. Distinctly Negroid, especially the mouth. The uraeus on the forehead is a sign of divinity. (See No. 47). 2. Venus of Willendorf. Woolly hair, breasts, hips, and labia majora like those of African Bushwoman. The face was probably painted on. (See Nos. 6 and 7). 3. Negro deity from Nicaragua, Central America. Probably tens of thousands of years old. (From American Museum of Natural History). 4. Negro idols from prehistoric Mexico. 5. Gigantic head of Negro god from Hueyapan, Mexico, one of the oldest known representations of a human being in the New Yorld. (See No. 16). All are indisputable proof of the Negro's great antiquity, and that he did not start as a slave to white people.

100 AMAZING FACTS ABOUT THE NEGRO

WITH COMPLETE PROOF

A Short Cut to The World History of The Negro

by

J. A. ROGERS

as well as additional information by the author and a biographical sketch by Helga M. Rogers

Author "From Superman to Man," "World's Greatest Men and Women of Color," "Sex and Race," etc., etc.

BRAWTLEY PRESS

Bay Street, St. Johns ANU

Copyright © 1995
HELGA M. ROGERS

ISBN: 978-1-943138-01-2

J.A. Rogers was born on September 6, 1880 in Negril, Parish Westmoreland, Jamaica, British West Indies to Samuel Rogers, a school teacher and Methodist minister, and Emily Johnstone. Emily bore Samuel four children, Joel Augustus, Martin, Ivy and Oswald. When I once asked him, where he got the name Joel, his answer was: "Simple, Joel was Samuel's first son in the Old Testament." Joel's mother died in 1886 in Buff Bay, of dysentery, about a month after the birth of Oswald. A grieving widower, "crying and all broken up" Samuel soon moved to St. Ann's Bay, where he met and courted his second wife, who bore him another seven children, the first one born in May 1888. In the meantime, Ivy, born in 1884, was sent to live with her maternal grandmother, who had a girls' school in Savanna-La-Mar. Ivy did not cherish that experience, remembering her grandmother as stern and very hard on her. Samuel moved from school to school, always trying to better his financial situation. In the end, he became the manager of a large plantation, Stetten. When we were in Jamaica in 1965, Joel remembered the location exactly, recognizing the roads leading to it, but the estate itself was gone. Joel remembered his stepmother not unkindly. He felt that she had treated her stepchildren well, "according to her lights", but that "her love was for her own children" and Joel and his brother Martin were none too pleased when they saw her pregnant again and again—"now, there will be even less affection for us." The problem, the way Joel saw it, was with his father, who was excessively stern with the boys, down to the youngest, Ian, born in 1900, while the girls remembered a different side of their father.

Anyway, his father had an education, as had his uncle Henry, a surveyor, while with eleven children, all Samuel could do for his own children was to be sure they had a good basic education. Joel never forgave him for that, nor that he did not give him much guidance. However his uncle Henry had a large library and Joel read, and read, and read.

After failing to get a scholarship for college, Joel joined the British Army and served with the Royal Garrison Artillery at Port Royal. When his unit was about to be transferred abroad, a medical examination revealed a heart murmur, and Joel was considered unfit for foreign service. By chance he met a friend in Kingston, who told him that his brother had emigrated to the United States and liked it there. Joel decided to go.

While the Jamaica of his day was quite color conscious, Joel did not think of himself in terms of color, but rather in terms of class. His father had not allowed him to play with the black children on the plantation; after all, he came from a family of status, light-skinned, with household help. It therefore came as a great shock when in the New York City of 1906 he was discriminated against in a Times Square greasy spoon. The rage and humiliation he must have felt were still evident as he retold the story throughout his life. He had a number of jobs in New York City—as a delivery man—and worked briefly in a bookstore in Montclair, NJ, where he was introduced as "our latest arrival from Cuba"—he was being passed as white since Jamaicans were considered, regardless of complexion, colored. (He did not like that and eventually went to Canada.) However, in the New York of 1906 he loved Coney Island, and in later years liked to go there at least once a year. He also enjoyed the cartoon, "The Katzenjammer Kids" which was popular at the time.

Joel went to Chicago, where he studied commercial art for nine years, supporting himself as a Pullman porter, only to discover that the only work open to him, even after getting "A-honorable mention" for his work, was as a housepainter. He remained a Pullman porter, which paid well, gave him the opportunity to visit the 48 states, and to meet many interesting people until he moved back to New York.

Some of his experiences as a Pullman porter were fictionalized in FROM "SUPERMAN" TO MAN. Although fictional, the historical facts are true. I have always felt that you hear his voice, meet the man, mentioning all the books he read, the authors, the art he saw. He had been reading all his life, had been deeply impressed by Dumas, by Victor Hugo's *Les Miserables*, by Plutarch's *Lives of Illustrious Greeks and Romans* and had studied the works of Schopenhauer for ten years. He identified with Schopenhauer's feeling that Human goodness consists of treating others with consideration, sympathy, and generosity, that goodness consists of treating the welfare and rights of others as important as one's own rights.

Joel became a naturalized citizen in 1917 and published the first edition of FROM "SUPERMAN" TO MAN the same year. By that time he was serious about his mission, the research into the origins of the human race, had found out that to be accomplished you did not have to have to be "white" in the American definition of the word. Also, most importantly, that slavery was not an inherently black condition or fate, that slavery had been around throughout recorded history.

During his early years in the States, he helped several of his siblings with their passage to the States. He was friendly with all of them but one has to understand that he was a man with a mission, which they did not share. Their concerns in life were different from his. They had families, they had livings to make, lived in white neighborhoods and can certainly not be blamed if they were less than eager to listen to his latest findings in his research all the time. "Passing" or not had nothing to do with that, very much apart from the fact that in surroundings divorced from his research he question of his color or lack thereof did not enter either. However, having had the early experience of his father siring eleven children, and the emotional deprivation he felt, he was a confirmed bachelor for most of his life. Also, with the sheer volume of his work, his books, his pamphlets, his articles, the fact that he travelled so extensively and lived for long stretches at a time in Paris—there really was no room in his life for a wife for most of his life.

Joel moved to New York City in 1921, where he met George S. Schuyler, who became his lifelong friend. He began to write for all the important Negro publications of his day, i.e. *The Messenger, The Pittsburgh Courier, The Amsterdam News*—writing for the latter two until his death in 1966. He also met H.L. Mencken and wrote for *American Mercury*.

Even in the 1920's, George Schuyler states in his book BLACK AND CONSERVATIVE that Joel had a tremendous knowledge of the historical background of the Negro and especially the miscegenation around the world. He took his first trip to Europe in 1925. He went to Paris, in 1927 to Germany, in 1928 to Egypt, in 1930 back to Paris and also to Ethiopia, where as a correspondent for The Amsterdam News he covered the coronation of Ras Tafari as he became the Emperor Haile Selassie . In 1935 he went back to Ethiopia to cover the Abyssinian War. Over the years, while retaining a residence in New York, with the exception of World War II, he made Paris his headquarters, doing his research from there, at the Biblioteque Nationale, at the British Museum in London, in Copenhagen, Oslo, Stockholm, Berlin, spending his time in museums, art galleries, antiquarian bookstores, churches. While in New York he went daily to the Rare Books Room in the NY Public Library.

Though Joel was an American citizen, he found life in Europe, especially in Paris, very congenial and gained recognition in France, as well as England early on. Recognition in the U.S. was much longer in coming and really quite spotty, though he did have his admirers, as I especially found out after his death. However, I never felt the recognition he had here was enough, considering the work he had done for others, helping to give them a leg up in the world and the intellectual wherewithal to do something with their lives. I always felt, and voiced it at the time, that had he used his brilliant mind and his dedication and tenacity for, say, cancer research, he would have had a Nobel Prize and the financial rewards, instead of the hand-to-mouth existence he lived most of his life, plus the lack of appreciation. While he did not disagree with my sentiments, he always felt that he would come into his own once he was gone, that he would be vindicated, which proved to be true. Anyway, he did what he wanted to do and lived the life he wanted to live, and he died a happy and fulfilled man.

He used his knowledge in his weekly columns in the *Pittsburgh Courier, The Amsterdam News, The Chicago Defender* and other publications. Thus he popularized Black history and he was recognized as an authority on the history of African people, on race and race relations. His columns on history were read by the general reader and were meant to give him a sense of self-worth and the feeling that he could become somebody in his own right and was not inferior to anyone. He fervently believed in the right to an equal chance at the starting gate of life, unencumbered with a sense of inferiority. He believed in one race, the human race, and that color was meaningless, and did not stand in the way of achievement. Thus "NATURE KNOWS NO COLOR LINE".

He made the attempt to locate Africa's proper place on the maps of human geography, he had found in his research that the Egypt of the pharaohs was not a White country by looking at Egyptian art. Egypt had a profound influence on Greece and not the other way around, that the White man's civilization was only a continuation of African civilizations of antiquity—all findings that did not make him very popular, but that have been validated in the meantime.

Charles Darwin predicted that the deepest roots of human evolution would be found in Africa. Joel also came across Dr. L.S. B. Leakey's research and find of fossils in the Olduvei Gorge in East Africa, proving that earliest man did indeed arise in Africa. Just recently a team of paleontologists from the University of California at Berkeley, led by Dr. Tim D. White, have broken a critical time barrier and found in Ethiopia the fossils of the oldest direct human ancestor, giving him the name Australopithecus ramidus.

As was generally the case, J. A. Rogers came across information , publicized it, was considered controversial and way off base in his statements and conclusions. Then subsequent research found him to be correct and could go beyond it, thereby validating it. Dr. Leslie C. Dunn of Columbia University, who was one of this country's leading geneticists, disproved the notion that the contribution of each parent blends in the child. These studies also have destroyed the old "blood theory" and contradict former views of fixed and absolute biological differences among the races. Geographic isolation, migration of populations and especially, mutations of genes have created "subgroups", Dr. Dunn argued, but these differences do not imply a basic difference of race. *(The New York Times*, 3/20/74)

Much was made in his Joel's lifetime in the States, though not in Europe, where he was recognized early on, of the fact that he was not a man of academic letters. That very much misses the point. He was a man who had learned idiomatic German, French and Spanish, could do his research in all these languages besides English and speak the languages fluently. He did the leg work and knew what to look for in his research. To try to evaluate his contribution to anthropology, racial origins, historical research in the light of today's basic academic requirements before anybody can get a foot in the door somewhere, is to look for Henry Ford's degree in Engineering, John D. Rockefeller's degree in Geology, etc. Advanced education was very rare at that time and that fact certainly neither stopped Henry Ford, nor Rockefeller, nor anybody else. Time marched on there, too, and today's cars are as far removed from the early cars, oil drilling has evolved greatly, and so on.

In his research all over the world, by looking at the artifacts first-hand, he compiled a body of history as a pioneer, with all the glories and drawbacks of a pioneer, decades ahead of his time, a work that will stand as his monument and will have to be referred to in any U.S. teaching of "integrated" history, integrated in the proper meaning of the word, history taught in its proper perspective, without trying to gloss over historical facts for one reason or another.

In his book AFRICA'S GIFT TO AMERICA, Joel stated that more than one half the world's cotton was grown by the Black man in the South by 1918. He perceived it as the Black man's crop. Professor Robert W. Fogel, who won the Nobel Memorial Prize in Economic Science for 1993 in Stockholm, wrote a book on slavery, "Time On The Cross", in 1974, in which he argued that the owners of slaves looked upon slaves as economic assets and treated them as well as livestock, that slavery was an efficient system for growing cotton and that the system collapsed for political—not economic reasons *(The New York Times*, October 13, 1993).

As John H. Clarke stated in his introduction to WORLD'S GREAT MEN OF COLOR, Vol. I, "In biographical research Rogers journeyed further and accomplished more than any other writer before him." Also, "in more than forty-five years of travel and research (two generations), he more than any other writer of his time, attempted to affirm the humanity of the African personality and to show the role that African people have played in the development of human history. This was singularly he major mission of his life, it was also the legacy that he left to his people and the world."

As the *New York Times Book Review* of February 4, 1973, written by John Ralph Willis had it, in reviewing WORLD'S GREAT MEN OF COLOR, "Rogers's reputation rests on two foundations. He brought African biography out of the backwater of world literature, and he removed the "Great Undiscussable" of sex-race as a formidable taboo for professional review."

He did more than anyone else in the field, and had his writings been heeded, maybe we would not have the awful mess with our schools, with the inner cities.

He married when he thought that he had most of his work completed and, therefore, a free mind for yet another adventure, marriage. However, AFRICA'S GIFT TO AMERICA as well as THE FIVE NEGRO PRESIDENTS were written subsequently. Still, he put as much effort into being a lovely husband as he had previously put into his work. He had a stroke while in Washington, D.C., where we visited friends. We had spent all day at the National Gallery and the Smithsonian Institution, where he found interesting things for his new book. He planned to go back to the Library of Congress the next week, for further research on the OLMECS. While he had established long ago that there had been migration from Africa to South America around 500 A.D., again something only validated after his lifetime, which accounted for some of the physiogonomies he found on the monuments, he wanted to write in depth about the OLMECS.........

He died on March 26, 1966 in New York. His work is his own monument to a brilliant, committed, highly idealistic man. To quote him, "...do we consider a man great because of the degree to which his life and actions affected humanity?"(World's Great Men of Color, Vol. I, How and Why This Book Was Written, p. 21). Using this criterion alone, he was a great man. Ave atque vale.

Helga Rogers
1995

"There are more things in heaven and earth than are dreamt of in your philosophy."—Shakespeare.

QUIZ

I. In what very important respect of population does the Aframerican differ now from all the other various groups of which the United States is composed, including the Indian, but is like the French, German, English, Belgian, and other peoples in Europe?

II. When did the seizure of a Negro woman as a slave in the United States lead to a war of two years in the United States in which 20.026 U. S. Army troops were engaged and during which a troop of 110 white soldiers, was led by a trusted Negro into a trap where all but four were massacred?

III. In what American State is marriage between white and black legal in one part of the State, and punishable with two years' imprisonment in the other part?

IV. A Negro girl saved George Washington from certain death at the beginning of the Revolution. Who was she?

V. When did Abraham Lincoln order back into slavery a half a million or more Negroes who had been declared free by one of his subordinates?

VI. What American vice-President because of his color and his features was publicly denounced in Congress and in the press as being a Negro?

VII. Beside the fact that the Thirteenth Amendment abolished slavery what most amazing fact is true of it?

100 AMAZING FACTS

1. The white population of New York is a third more illiterate than the Negro one.

2. Benjamin Banneker, a Negro astronomer, made the first clock made in America in 1754.

3. The word, "coffee", comes from Caffa, Ethiopia, where it was first used and where it still grows wild.

4. George Washington sent a Negro slave to Barbados to be exchanged for a hogshead of molasses, a cask of rum and "other good old spirits", in 1776.

5. The Negro arrived in the New World free from tuberculosis, and syphilis, or other venereal disease. Livingstone, the famous African missionary, and a medical doctor says, Syphilis "dies out in the African interior. It seems incapable of permanence in any form in persons of pure African blood." Syphilis originated in Europe in 1494, when there was a great epidemic of it. As this was two years after the discovery of the New World, it was erroneously believed to have been brought back by the sailors of Columbus.

THE ARTS

6. The Negro was the first artist. The oldest drawings and carvings yet discovered were executed by the Negro peoples over 15,000 years ago in Southern France, Northern Spain, Palestine, South Africa, and India. The drawings are on rocks, the carvings on bone; basalt and ivory.

7. The oldest known representation of the human body is that of a Negro woman It was carved by a Negro sculptor of Grimaldi race from 10,000 to 15,000 years ago. It is called "The Venus of Willendórf" after the place in Austria where it was found, and is in the Vienna Museum.

8. Beethoven, the world's greatest musician, was without a doubt a dark mulatto. He was called "The Black Spaniard." His teacher, the immortal Joseph Haydn, who wrote the music for the former Austrian National Anthem, was colored, too.

9. Jose Vasconcelos (El Negrito Poeta), born of African Congo parents at Almolonga, Mexico, about 1710, wrote verses that were so popular that they entered into Mexican folk-lore and were printed annually on the calendars of Mexico until 1872, one hundred and twelve years after his death.

ANCIENT CIVILIZATIONS

10. The Grimaldi, a Negro race, lived in Europe as late as 12,000 years ago. Two complete Grimaldi skeletons are in the Museum of Monaco, near Monte Carlo. Abundant traces of their culture have been unearthed in Southern and Central Europe.

11. Elam, a mighty Negro civilization of Persia, flourished about 2900 B. C. and is perhaps older than Egypt or Ethiopia. One of its later Negro kings, Kudur Nakunta, conquered Chaldea and Babylon and brought back to his capital, Susa, rich treasures among which was the famous statue of the goddess, Nana. Later it became the capital of Cyrus the Great and Darius. Susa is the Shushan of the Bible where Esther, the Jewess, sought the favor of King Ahaserus of Persia and Ethiopia.

12. Cheops, a Negro, built the Great Pyramid, one of the Seven Wonders of the Ancient World. It is 451 feet high, has 2,500,000 blocks of granite, each two and a half tons, covers 13 acres, took 100,000 men thirty years to build and was completed in 3730 B. C.

13. There were at least eighteen Ethiopian or unmixed Negro rulers of Ancient Egypt, the best known of which is Piankhi. Leaving his country in Central Africa, Piankhi conquered all Egypt to the mouth of the Nile in 750 B. C.

14. The Ganges, the sacred river of India, is named after an Ethiopian king of that name who conquered Asia as far as this river.

15. The most ancient lineage in the world is that of the Ethiopian royal family. It is said to be older than that of King George VI's by 6130 years. The Emperor Haile Selassi I, ruler of Ethiopia, traces his ancestry to King Solomon and the Queen of Sheba and beyond that to Cush, 6280 B. C.

16. Negroes lived in America thousands of years before Columbus. Central American monuments show numerous carving of them as gods. When Columbus came to the New World, Negroes had been crossing from Africa to South America a distance of 1600 miles. The first white men to reach the American mainland, tell of seeing Negroes. Columbus who visited South America said that he had heard of them there.

17. The present Negro race of Africa perhaps did not originate there, but Asia and Oceania. The earliest inhabitants of Africa were not black but brown. Today the peoples of mixed and unmixed Negro descent living in Asia and Oceania probably exceed in number the present Negro population of Africa. India has millions of Negroes. The purest Negro types are in Southern Asia. In 1923, Dr. Joseph Rock, United States Department of Agriculture discovered a hitherto unknown Negro race, the Nakhis, 200,000 in number, in Southern China. In 1934, E. W. P. Chinnery discovered an unknown Negro people in New Guinea, near Australia. He reports that they have a civilization superior to their neighbors, who live under white rule.

18. In the United States Army Drafts in World War I, the Negro proved physically fitter than the white man. "For every 100 men physically examined the ratio of colored men found physioally qualified for general military service was substantially higher than the ratio of the white men by just five per cent, namely 74.60 against 69.71."

ILLITERACY AND INTELLIGENCE

19. The peoples of Southern Europe, including Italy, and most of those of Eastern Europe, including Russia, are more illiterate than the Negroes of the United States. In seventy years Negro illiteracy has fallen off about 80 per cent. In 1870 it was 82 per cent; in 1930, 16.3.

20. Aframerican illiteracy, is three times higher than the white one, nevertheless, when certain states are matched against certain others, there are surprising comparisons. For instance, the Negroes of California, Minnesota, New York, Nevada, South Dakota, Oregon and Washington are less illiterate than the Native Whites of White parentage in Virginia, West Virginia, North Carolina, South Carolina, Georgia, Kentucky, Tennessee, Alabama, Arkansas, Louisiana, and New Mexico. New York, Minnesota, Oregon, and South Dakota Negroes are less illiterate than Mississippi Whites. The Negroes of these seven states are less illiterate by 100 to 400 per cent than the foreign-born Whites of all the States, save one.

21. In the United States Army Intelligence tests during World War I, the Negroes of Pennsylvania, New York, Illinois and Ohio led the Whites of Mississippi, Kentucky, Arkansas and Georgia by from one to seven per cent.

22. Two centuries ago the Negroes of South Africa and the Northern Europeans both practised a form of cannibalism that was strikingly similar. Of the vital organs of slain foes, the Negroes made a muti, or charm, against evil. Sometimes they ate the heart of a brave man believing that it gave added courage. The Europeans would roast or dry the bodies of hanged criminals. Of these they made mumia, a medicine for internal and external use, which was supposed to have peculiar curative charm. In 1683 when the Germans defeated the Turks at Ofen, Switzerland, thousands of surrendered Turks were treated in this manner. An army surgeon, who was present, wrote: "None were given grace. All were massacred, and in most cases they were skinned, the fatty parts were roasted, and the genitals cut off, dried, and put into big sacks. And of this they made precious mumia." Regular cannibalism existed in Germany as late as 1650.

EXPLORATION

23. Estevanico, a Negro from Morocco, was one of a party of four to cross the North American continent in 1536 for the first time. The journey took nine years. In 1539 he headed an expedition that discovered Arizona and New Mexico. Estevanico's travels served to open up the Southwest and the States west of Florida, as far as the Pacific.

24. The founder of the City of Chicago was Baptist Pointe de Saible, a Negro, in 1779.

25. Tippoo Tib, a Negro trader in slaves and ivory, from Zanibar, East Africa, was the first civilized man to penetrate the center of Africa. He explored territory nearly as large as the United States. Stanley, Weismann, Cameron, and other white explorers followed in his path. He died in 1905, very rich.

26. For 2234 years human beings had been trying to reach the top of the world. Thousands of lives and millions of dollars were lost in the attempt. On April 6, 1909, Matthew Henson, a New York Negro, was the first of a party of six to do so. He is now (1943) the only human being alive to have stood there The first Arctic explorer was Pytheas, a Greek, who perished in the attempt in 325 B. C.

SCIENCE AND INVENTION

27. Jan Ernest Matzeliger, a Dutch West Indian Negro living in Lynn, Mass., invented the first machine for sewing the soles of shoes to the uppers. This invention, which was eleven years in the making, revolutionized the industry and gave shoe supremacy to the United States. It made several millionaires, one of whom left $4,000,000 to Harvard University. Overwork and privation hastened Matzeliger to his grave in 1889 at the age of 37. He left a few shares of stock to a white church, which later saved it from being sold for debt.

28. George Washington Carver of Tuskegee Institute, one of the world's greatest agricultural chemists, was awarded the Roosevelt Medal in 1939 for "distinguished service in the field of science." From the peanut he has extracted 285 products, and from the sweet potato, 118. Dr. Carver was born a slave. Thomas Edison once offered him a large salary to take charge of one of the Edison laboratories but Carver refused in order to continue the work he had begun with Booker T. Washington at Tuskegee Institute.

JEWS AND ETHIOPIANS

29. The Mohammedans believe that Moses was a black man. Their Bible, The Koran, says so. God told Moses to put his hand into his bosom. The Koran says that it came out white. The commentators declare that Moses' hand could not have been white before, and that the miracle Jehovah intended was making the black skin white, and then turning it black again. The Septuagint, or Greek Bible, agrees with the Koran.

30. The characters of the Bible are largely Negroes. The Jews were slaves to the Egyptians for nearly 430 years. Only seventy Jews went to Egypt with Jacob. The Bible says that 600,000 men left with Moses, which according to Haushoffer, meant a total of 3,154,000 with women and children. For this large number to have left mixing with the Egyptians, who were black, must have taken place on a vast scale. About 12,000,000 Negroes were brought to the New World. Imagine how much of their original color and culture the latter would take with them should they "return" to Africa, and you realize how much of the original Jew remained in only those seventy Jews after four centuries. Tacitus, Roman historian of 90 A.D., says that the Romans of his day popularly believed that the Jews, which then abounded in Europe, came from Ethiopia, the land of the Blacks. The present white color of the European and American Jew, is very likely due to the same cause, as the fair skin and straight hair of large numbers of Negroes." The Bible classes the Ethiopian and the Jew together, "Are ye not as the children of Ethiopia unto me, O children of Israel, saith the Lord." Chaldea, the land in which the Jews originated, was also a Negro land, hence Abraham might also have been black.

31. The Falashas, or Negro Jews of Ethiopia, led by Queen Judith, put the line of Solomon and the Queen of Sheba off the throne of Ethiopia in 937 A. D., and ruled for forty years. The Falashas assert that they are the original Jews. They call themselves "The Beta-Israel," or "The Chosen People."

32. The Negro Jews of India are not permitted to enter the same synagogues as the white ones, nor to bury their dead in the same cemeteries.

MEDICINE

33. Imhotep of Ancient Egypt, was the real Father of Medicine. He lived about 2300 B. C. Greece and Rome had their knowledge of medicine from him. In Rome he was worshipped as the Prince of Peace in the form of a black man. His Ethiopian portraits show him a Negro. Imhotep was also Prime Minister to King Zoser as well as the foremost architect of his time. The saying, "Eat, drink, and be merry for tomorrow we die," has been traced to him. Hippocrates, the so-called "Father of Medicine" lived 2,000 years after Imhotep.

34. Aben Ali, an African Negro, was private physician to Charles VII, King of France (1403-1465). When the king fell dangerously ill at Toulouse, Aben Ali was sent for and he cured him. Thereafter the king made him a member of his suite.

35. Dr. C. Tavares, an African Negro, was the private physician to King Carlos I of Portugal until the latter's death in 1908.

36. Dr. Daniel Williams, Chicago surgeon who died in 1931, was the first to perform a successful operation on the human heart.

POLITICS

37. France has had six colored Cabinet Ministers—Severiano de Heredia, 1887; Senator Henri Lemery, 1915-1918, and 1934; Alcide Delmont, 1928; Blaise Diagne, 1931; Gratien Candace, 1932; Gaston Monnerville, 1937. De Heredia, as Minister of Public Works, built some of France's finest roads.

38. Eugene Chen, one of the most dynamic political figures of the present century, and Minister of Foreign Affairs for China in 1927, was born of Chinese-Negro parentage in Trinidad, West Indies, in 1878. He was also secretary to Dr. Sun Yat Sen, first president of China.

RACE-MIXING

39. Persina, a Queen of Ethiopia, 60 B. C., presented her husband, Hydaspes, with a light-colored child, "which color is strange among Ethiopians." She declared that it was due to the presence of a white statue in the room at the time of conception. Similarly Maria Theresa of Spain and Austria, wife of Louis XIV, King of France, bore him a mulatto daughter in 1665. The Queen, spent most of her time with a Negro dwarf, named Nabo, while the King passed most of his with the beauties that thronged his court. The doctors explained the color of the child by saying that the black man looked at the Queen. "It must have been a very penetrating look," said the King, wrathfully. A noted writer of that time attributed the color of a similar child, born to a high noblewoman, to the mother's fondness for chocolate.

40. Anna, a Negro servant girl of Calavecchio, Italy, wife of a white mule-driver, became the concubine of Pope Clement VII. Her son, Alessandro, born 1511, became reigning Duke of Florence, and married Margaret, only daughter of the Emperor Charles V, ruler of Germany, the Netherlands, Austria, and Spain in 1536.

41. White American slave-holders used to induce white women to marry Negro slaves in order to hold the women slaves for life.

42. Thomas Jefferson, third president of the United States, and father of the Declaration of Independence, was the father of a large number of mulatto children. His wife protested loud and long to no avail. Patrick Henry, another signer of that document, had a Negro son named Melancthon.

43. Napoleon planned to solve the color problem in Haiti by making it legal for each man to take three wives, one white, one mulatto, the other black. He had several conferences with the theologians on "this grand measure," and tried to win the consent of the Pope.

44. In 1787 while a party of 351 freed Negroes was aboard ship at Portsmouth, England, enroute to Sierra Leone, West Africa, the authorities brought on board sixty-two white women, prostitutes and others, whom they wished to get rid of, and married them to as many men, and sent them off to be the future mothers of the colony.

45. In the 1850's, Mrs. Leybonn, an Englishwoman, was "Queen of the Slave-traders," at Rio Pongo, one of the principal slave posts in West Africa. She had a fort armed with cannon and armed by 300 devoted blacks. She had three mulatto children by a Negro, a boy and two girls. One of the latter married a white slave-trader, and the other, a British Consul.

46. The Countess de Beauharnais, who was related by marriage to Napoleon, married a full-blooded Haitian Negro, named Castaing, who was a member of the Paris Convention of 1792-1795.

RELIGION

47. The oldest and most noted statue in the world bears the face of a Negro. It is the Sphinx of Gizeh, which was worshipped as Horus, or Harmachis, the Sun-God of Light and Life. It was erected about 5,000 B. C.

The Devil which is now depicted as black, was once portrayed as White. When the black man dominated the planet he painted the forces of evil, white.

When the whites came into power they shifted the colors. But as late as 1500 the Ethiopians still depicted their gods and heroes black, and their devils and villains, white. Father Fernandez, a Catholic missionary, who worked amongst them at this time, says, "They paint Christ, the Blessed Virgin, and other saints in black form; and devils and wicked men, white. Thus Christ and his apostles are black and Judas, white. Annas, Caiphas, Pilate, Herod and the Jews are white, while Michael is black, and the Devil, white."

48. Nearly all of the ancient gods of the Old and New World were black and had woolly hair. Buckley says, "From the woolly texture of the hair I am inclined to assign to the Buddha of India; the Fuhi of China; the Xaha of the Japanese; and the Quetzalcoatl of the Mexicans, the same and indeed an African, or rather, a Nubian origin." In the Bible, God, or the Ancient of Days, is described as having "hair like the pure wool." The earliest statues of the Virgin Mary and Christ in Europe as far north as Russia, were black and Negroid.

49. The Bible really originated in Ancient Egypt, where the population, according to Herodotus and Aristotle, was black. Here the Jews received almost all of their early culture. Prof. Breasted, leading Egyptologist, says, "The ripe social and moral development of mankind in the Nile Valley which is 3000 years older than that of the Hebrews, contributed essentially to the formation of Hebrew literature. Our moral heritage therefore derives from a wider human past enormously older than the Hebrews, and it has come to us rather THROUGH the Hebrews than FROM them."

50. Psalms that read like those of the Bible were written by a Pharaoh, Amenophis IV, better known as "Akhenaton, the Heretic King," 1300 B. C. or more than 400 years before David was born. Akhenaton, who was the father of Tut-Ankh-Amen, was extremely Negro in type. He is called "the most remarkable of the Pharaohs."

51. Ethiopians, that is Negroes, gave to the world the first idea of right and wrong and thus laid the basis of religion, and of all true culture and civilization. The earliest exposition of this yet found is in the so-called Memphite Drama, which is known only through a copy on a slab of basalt made by order of an Ethiopian King in 700 B. C.

52. There were three African Popes of Rome: Victor (189-199 A. D.); Melchiades (311-312); and St. Gelasius (496 A. D.). It was Melchiades who led Christianity to final triumph against the Roman Empire.

53. The celestial saint of Germany is St. Maurice, a pure Negro. While in command of a Roman legion in Gaul (Switzerland), in 287 A. D., he refused to attack the Christians when ordered to do so by the Emperor Maximian Herculius, for which he was killed. His picture is in many German cathedrals and museums sometimes with the German eagle on his head. Recent pictures of Hitler, nearly 1700 years later, show Hitler also with the same emblem on his head.

RULERS

54. On November 15, 218 B. C., Hannibal, a full-blooded Negro, marching through conquered territory in Spain and France, performed the astounding feat of crossing the Alps. With only 26,000 of his original force of 82,000 men remaining, he defeated Rome, the mightiest military power of that age, who had a million men, in every battle for the next fifteen years.

Hannibal is the father of military strategy. His tactics are still taught in the leading military academies of the United States, England, France, Germany, and other lands.

55. Yusuf, a king from Upper Senegal, Africa, saved Moorish civilization in Spain in 1086. The Moors were being pushed out by the white Christians of Germanic descent. Yusuf crossed the Strait of Gibraltar with only 15,000 men, most of them pure blacks, and with 10,000 more from the Moors met the white king, Alphonso VI, at Zalacca. The latter had an army of 70,000, nearly three times as great, but Yusuf inflicted a terrific defeat on him. The flower of white knighthood was destroyed in that battle. Among those who fell later before the military prowess of Yusuf was Roderigo Diaz de Bivar, known as "The Cid," and the greatest figure of the heroic age of Spain.

56. In 1538, Askia The Great, Emperor of Songhay, ruled an empire that stretched from the Atlantic Ocean to Lake Chad, and larger than Western Europe. His capital was Timbuctoo.

57. The first World War in history was started by Abraha, Negro emperor and ex-slave, when he attacked Mecca, Arabia, in 569 A. D. This war lasted for more than a thousand years and stretched from France to beyond China. It brought about the fall, of several great empires, one of them the Later Roman Empire, capital Constantinople in 1453 A. D.

58. Muley Ismael, Emperor of Morocco, whose mother was a Negro slave, had 25,000 white slaves captured on the seas or on the coasts of Europe and the British Isles, to build his palace at Meknes. Muley Ismael's stables were the vastest in existence with stalls for 12,000 horses. Muley Ismael's ships raided the coasts of Europe for slaves until his death in 1727.

59. John VI, King of Portugal, a dark mulatto, was the maker of modern Brazil. Transferring his throne to Rio de Janeiro in 1808, he ruled Portugal from Brazil. This is the first and only time a European country has been ruled by an American one.

60. Pedro I, colored son of John VI, became first emperor of Brazil in 1822. Pedro I married the sister of Napoleon's second wife. Gloria, Pedro's daughter, became Queen of Portugal and was a sister-in-law of Victoria, Queen of England. Many members of European royalty trace their ancestry to the Negro ruler, John VI.

61. Jean Baptiste Bernadotte, a colored man, was the founder of the present royal family of Sweden. Enlisting as a private in Napoleon's army he rose to be field-marshal. In 1818 he ascended to the throne of Sweden as Charles XIV.

62. Cetewayo, King of Zululand, South Africa, massacred an entire British army sent against him in 1879, and a few days later defeated and killed the Prince Napoleon, heir to the French throne. Cetewayo taught the Europeans the skirmish line in warfare.

SLAVERY

63. The word, "slave," was originally applied to white people. It comes from "Slav," a Russian people captured by the Germans.

64. The first slaves held in the United States were not black, but white. They were Europeans, mostly British, who died like flies on the slave-ships across. On one voyage 1,100 perished out of 1,500. At another time 350 out of 400. In Virginia, white servitude was for a limited period, but was sometimes extended to life. In the West Indies, particularly in the case of the Irish, it was for life. White people were sold in the United States up to 1826, fifty years after the signing of the Declaration of Independence. Andrew Johnson, President of the United States, was a runaway, and was advertised for in the newspapers.

65. Between 1526 and 1859 there were thirty-three slave revolts in the United States, one of which was that headed by Nat Turner of Virginia in 1831. With only six companions Turner set out to free the 3,000,000 slaves. The United States marines and two warships were sent against him after he had killed 55 whites, and captured several plantations. The Seminoles, or runaways of mixed Indian and Negro descent, of Florida, fought three wars with the United States to preserve their freedom.

66. In 1670, Virginia passed a law forbidding Negroes from buying white people. This was fifty-one years after the Negro had arrived in chains. The same law was repeated in 1748. Free Negroes bought white people in such numbers in Louisiana, that the state made a similar law in 1818.

67. White children were kidnapped in the British Isles at the rate of several thousands yearly in the 17th and 18th Centuries and sold into slavery in America and the West Indies. Sometimes they were bootlegged and sold as Negroes. White Americans, North and South, were also kidnapped or seduced and sold as Negroes as late as 1859. One of the most celebrated cases of a white person sold as a Negro was Sally Muller, who was held in servitude in Louisiana for twenty-six years. Court after court ruled against her. Finally her birth certificate was dug up in Germany and she was freed by the Supreme Court in 1818.

68. Prince Abd-El-Rahman, a highly educated grandson of the Emperor of Timbuctoo, was captured in battle and sold into slavery in America. Years later a white doctor, who had travelled in his land, saw him at Natchez, Miss. Rahman was freed in 1829. $4,000 was paid for the liberation of his children.

69. In 1860 there were 487,000 free Negroes in the United States some of whom owned slaves. C. D. Wilson estimates that there were 6,230 Negro slave-holders. The tax returns of Charleston, S. C., for 1860 showed 132 Negro slave-holders with 390 slaves. The Negro slave-holders, like the white ones, fought to keep their chattels in the Civil War.

70. The Brazilian Emancipation Proclamation of 1888 freed all the slaves on the day of promulgation; the British Emancipation of 1834, not until four years later; while the American Emancipation Proclamation of 1863 when issued "freed" those slaves whom Abraham Lincoln had no power to free, and permitted the continued enslavement of those whom he had the power to free.

71. In Arabia and parts of North Africa, white persons, mostly women, are still held as slaves as are many Negroes. Sometimes the owners of these white slaves are Negroes.

SPORTS

72. The fastest bicyclist the world has ever known was Marshall (Major) W. Taylor. He defeated the champions of Europe and America. His greatest feat was the winning of the one-mile motor-paced race in 1 minute, 19 seconds. He died in 1932 at the age of 54.

73. The Aframerican, though but a dot in the world's population holds, or has held an unusually high percentage of world athletic championships. There have been thirteen world boxing champions. Jack Johnson and Joe Louis, heavyweight; John Henry Lewis, light heavyweight; Tiger Flowers, middleweight; Joe Walcott, Dixie Kid, Jack Thompson, welterweight; Henry Armstrong, three titles, welterweight, lightweight, bantamweight; Joe Gans, lightweight; George Dixon, two titles, bantamweight and featherweight.

Negroes have held ten Olympic titles: De Hart Hubbard, broad jump, 1924; Eddie Tolan, two titles, 100 metres and 200 metres, 1932; Ed Gordon, broad jump, 1932; Cornelius Johnson, high jump, 1936; Jesse Owens, three titles, 100 and 200 metres and broad jump, 1936; John Woodruff, 800 metres, 1936; Archie Williams, 400 metres, 1936.

National and university titles, and world record-breaking titles, in sports have been held by the hundreds. Of 12 inter-collegiate championships competed for on June 1, 1940, Negroes won eight.

WARFARE — COMMANDERS

74. The Rock of Gibraltar, the symbol of stability, is named after a Negro ex-slave. It is a corruption of "Gebal-Tarik," or "The Mountain of Tarik." Tarik, who was a Moor, captured the Rock which was then called Calpe, in 711 A. D. Later he conquered Southern Spain. Tarik's countrymen thereafter ruled Spain for 700 years.

75. Abraham Hannibal, captured as a slave in Africa, was adopted by Peter the Great as his son and taught military engineering. Later Hannnibal became tutor to the heir to the throne, and commander-in-chief of the Russian army. He died in 1782 at the age of 90, owning vast estates and 2000 white slaves.

76. Toussaint L'Ouverture and his great mulatto rival, General Rigaud, were both thrown into the same dungeon in France by Napoleon in 1802. Later at St. Helena, Napoleon declared that the imprisonment of Toussaint was a grave political error.

77. Toussaint L'Ouverture had planned after Haiti was freed to go to Dahomey, West Africa, and use it as a base from which to fight the slave-trade. For this purpose he saved 6,000,000 gold francs, equivalent to that sum in dollars now, which he entrusted to Stephen Girard, an American ship captain. After the treacherous capture of Toussaint, Girard would not turn over this money to Toussaint's family. During his nine months' imprisonment Toussaint was tormented by Napoleon's agents to reveal the hiding-place of the money. Later Girard, a Frenchman by birth, became the richest American of his day. He left millions on his death in 1831 for the founding of Girard College in Philadelphia, stipulating that it should be for whites only. He also gave money to buy coal for the poor of Philadelphia, with the same provision.

78. Jean Francois, leader of the Haitian blacks in 1791, an ex-slave and once superior officer of Toussaint L'Ouverture, rose to be a grandee of Spain. This gave him the privilege of calling the king of Spain "cousin," and wearing his hat in the royal presence. He was a favorite at the Court of Madrid.

79. Napoleon had twelve West Indian Negro generals, who served in France, namely: General Alexander Dumas, once Napoleon's superior officer; Andre Rigaud; Martial Besse; B. Leveille; Antoine Cloualatte; J. B. Belley; Magloire Pelage; Alex. Petion; A. Chanlatte; Barthelmy; Villate; and Etienne V. Mentor.

80. Mohammed Ahmed, called the Mahdi, an ex-waiter of the Sudan, defeated every army that England sent against him, one of which was 11,000 strong. At his death in 1885, he had carved out for himself an empire in Africa, 1600 miles long and 700 miles wide. Among those killed by the Mahdi was the famous English General, "Chinese" Gordon.

81. One of the most daring leaders of the Filipinos against the American troops in the Philippines in 1899 was an American Negro deserter, named Fagan. A short story based on his life by Rowland Thomas, noted American writer, won first prize of $10,000 in a nation-wide contest in 1914.

82. General A. Dodds, a Senegalese, was France's best known soldier, prior to the first World War. In 1901, as the senior general he commanded for a brief time the Allied Army—white Americans, Germans, British, French, and Japanese—against the Boxers in China. The Germans, unable to tolerate that, hurriedly sent out a field-marshal.

83. Captain of the Navy S. H. Mortenol, an unmixed Negro, commanded the Air Defenses of Paris from 1916-1918, with 205 planes and 10,000 white men under him. It was he who located and destroyed the Big Berthas that used to bombard Paris from a distance of sixty to eighty miles.

84. The leader of the last successful Cuban revolt in 1933 was Fulgencio Batista, a Negro sergeant from Oriente Province, who was later President of the Republic.

WARFARE — MEN

85. The United States has had seven big wars, exclusive of Indian ones. The Negro has distinguished himself in all of them. In the last war, France awarded the Croix de Guerre to four whole Negro regiments, the 369th, 370th, 371st and 372nd, as well as to the first battalion of the 367th. Sixty Negro officers and 350 non-commissioned officers and men were decorated for valor. Forty-one Negroes have received the Congressional Medal of Honor for bravery.

86. In the American Civil War, the Negro played a role similar to that of America in the last World War. That is, both provided a balance of power that brought victory to one side. Without the aid of the Negro, there might have been no United States now. Abraham Lincoln said four times that without the Negro it would be "impossible" for the North to win. This statement is all the more striking since Lincoln, in response to popular prejudice, steadfastly refused at first to employ Negro troops though the South was doing so. Instead, he wanted to ship the Negroes away and in 1862 had Congress to vote $600,000 to send the first instalment to the Ile de Vache in Haiti. The colony ended in disastrous failure and Lincoln sent a ship for the surviving Negro deportees.

87. 178,975 Negro soldiers fought in the Union Army between 1861-1865. There were 161 Negro regiments as follows: 141 infantry; 7 cavalry; 12 heavy artillery; and 1 light artillery. The total number of Negroes aiding the Union Army was perhaps twice that number.

88. The number of free Negroes in the United States, who fought to perpetuate slavery is not exactly known, but there must have been thousands. In June, 1861, Tennessee began to recruit Negroes between the ages of 18 and 50. South Carolina did the same in 1862. In a review of 28,000 Confederate troops held at New Orleans on November 23, 1861, seven months after the outbreak of war, there was one regiment of 1400 free Negroes. Preston Roberts, a Negro, was unofficial quartermaster of General Nathaniel Forrest. He was given the Cross of Honor, the highest Confederate medal, and until his death in 1910 was treated in all respects like a white man in the South.

89. The national hero of Buenos Aires, now the City of Buenos Aires, was Antonio Ruiz (El Negro Falucho), who died rather than let the rebels pull down the flag of Buenos Aires and hoist that of Spain on the night of February 3, 1810. A magnificent monument stands to his honor in that city.

90. The first two Americans to be decorated by France in the first World War were Henry Johnson, and Needham Roberts, both Negroes. Johnson killed four Germans and wounded twenty-eight others single-handed.

MISCELLANEOUS

91. The most ancient names for so-called black people are Nehesu, or Nubian; Ethiopian, and Moor from Ancient Egypt, and Negro or Nigrita from West Africa. All the above are native African words. "Negro" is probably the oldest as the Negritos are the oldest known branch of the human race. "Negro" comes from the River Niger. "Niger" found its way into Latin and since the people from that region were dark-skinned, Niger, nigra, nigrum came to mean black. Negro, Negrito, Nigrita, means "the people of the great river." Black and colored, like white, are, on the other hand, European words. Ethiopian and Moor were popularly used to describe the so-called blacks until 1500. Shakespeare uses "Negro" only once and uses it synonymously with Moor. Africa comes from the ancient Egyptian "Af-rui-ka," or Kafrica, the land of the Kaffir.

92. The English word, "admiral," and the French equivalent, "amiral," were adopted as the result of the great admiration held for the Negroid sea-rovers who used to scour the coasts of Europe for slaves as late as the 19th Century. It comes from Amir-al-Bahr (Lord of the Seas), the commander of the sea-rovers. The principal port of the latter was Salee, Morocco. A United States squadron, under Commodore Decatur, went to Africa to free the white Americans held there as slaves.

93. Ex-Kaiser Wilhelm II had a Negro "uncle" by adoption. His grandfather, Wilhelm I, adopted a Negro boy given him by an African explorer, as his son. Henri Noel, as he was called, grew up in the royal palace, and was an officer in the German army.

94. The chief Back-to-Africa leaders were: Paul Cuffee, Major Martin R. Delany, African explorer; "Pop" Singleton; William Ellis; Chief

Sam; Dr. Thorne; and Marcus Garvey. The last-named had a following much greater than the rest combined.

95. Tony Simpson, a humble Louisiana Negro, posing as Prince Antonio Apache of Arizona, became the social lion of the elite of New York and Philadelphia in 1903. Among those who feted him in their drawing rooms or in the Golden Horse-Shoe at the Metropolitan Opera were Mrs. John Jacob Astor, Mrs. Howard Gould, and Mrs. John R. Drexel. Even President Theodore Roosevelt was taken in. The latter consulted "Prince Apache," several times on Indian affairs at the White House. The "Prince" was tall and imposing, dressed like a Beau Brummel, and had the manners of a Chesterfield. He used to wear a wig attached to a tuft of his own woolly hair.

96. After his famous speech at the Atlanta Exposition in 1895, Booker T. Washington refused an offer of $50,000 for a series of lectures, because it would interrupt his work at Tuskegee, which was bringing him much less.

97. Haywood Shepherd, a free Negro, was the first person killed by John Brown's party of white and Negro raiders at Harper's Ferry in their efforts to free the slaves in 1859. Shepherd, while running off to arouse the white people, was shot dead in his tracks.

98. The blacks, like the whites, have been struggling for thousands of years to change their hair from its natural form. Negroes arranged their hair with hot irons in Egypt more than 5,000 years ago.

99. An American Negro has twenty chances to a white American's one of reaching a hundred years and over.

100. Since 1460 A. D. or earlier, the Negroes of Seville, Spain, had been wearing in the religious procession on the feast of Corpus Cristi, a white robe and hood, strikingly like that used by the Ku Klux Klan, which originated 428 years later.

PROOF

In presenting proof of the "100 AMAZING FACTS ABOUT THE NEGRO," I felt that it would not be enough to say that I had met this or that person or seen this or that thing in a museum or an ancient ruin. I have tried rather to give recorded proof, that is, a book in which they were mentioned. Books in foreign languages were cited only when there were no English translations at all, or such translations were poor or abridged.

Of pictures, which will be even more convincing, I have a large number. Among them are St. Maurice; the coins of Hannibal of Carthage; the Negro Buddhas, Christs, and Virgin Marys; Delphos, founder of the great Delphic oracle of Greece, the Negro daughter of Maria Theresa, Queen of France; Negro gods in America before Columbus, and a collection of very Negroid rulers of Egypt, all of which, together with several hundred other noted Negroes, may be seen in "Sex and Race, Vols. I, II and III.

ANSWERS TO QUIZ

1. The Aframerican group has a greater percentage of women than men. In 1930 there were 1027 white men for every 1000 white women and only 970 Negro men for every 1000 colored women. The 1930 census says, "Differing from all other races the Negroes have shown an excess of females at every census since and including that of 1840....The relative excess of females in 1930 was greater than that shown at any previous census except that of 1870....The Indian population has shown an excess of males." (Vol. II, p. 94.)

The effect of this is far-reaching and significant. Since the birthrate of a population is determined, not by the percentage of males, but of the females, the Negro group is assured of a greater proportionate increase than any of the white groups, the more so as white immigration has been greatly reduced.

Again the shortage of white women means that white men will continue to seek Negro women, hence, that laws or conventions against intermarriage are a direct creator of concubinage and immorality and will be as long as the Negro women remain economically weak.

Another deduction is that despite popular belief the Negro women are not less moral than the white ones, as a group. For instance, European women are more chaste than American ones, not because of any inherent quality, but because there are less men to pursue them. Like the Aframerican, the European nations have an excess of females. Thus since there is a shortage of men vast numbers of European women must remain continent whether they will or not.

The actual fact, according to the latest official report, is that the native white women, as a whole, were less moral than the Negro or the foreign-born white women. Among the eight offenses in which the native white women led all the other groups are, "Fornication and prostitution....keeping house of ill-fame and adultery"....(Bureau of Census, Prisoners, 1923, p. 68).

The very high Negro infant death-rate offsets the high Negro birthrate. Large numbers of bleached-out Negroes also drift away annually into the white group. But with the Aframericans having the advantage of this high percentage of women, the theory that the Negro race in the United States will disappear in a century is entirely without foundation.

II. In 1836, the Negro wife of Osceola, a Seminole chief of Indian-Negro descent was seized as a slave. Osceola, in revenge, ambushed, killed and scalped U. S. General Thompson, and three other white men. Thus began the Second Seminole War. Osceola, says J. R. Giddings, "visited Fort King in company with his wife and a few friends for the purpose of trading. Mr. Thompson, the Agent, was present and while engaged in business the wife of Osceola was seized as a slave. Evidently having Negro blood in her veins the law pronounced her a slave and as no other person could show title to her the pirate who had got possession of her body was supposed, of course, to be her owner....Osceola became frantic with rage....From that moment when this outrage was committed the Florida War may be regarded as commenced."

The trusted Negro guide who deliberately led Col. Dade into the trap where he and all his men, save four, were massacred is Louis Pacheco. (The Exiles of Florida, p. 98, 101, 106, 114). For fuller details of the campaign, the number of men engaged and killed, see J. T. Sprague: The Florida War, New York, 1848.

III. In the part of Colorado settled by Mexico marriage between white and black is legal; in that settled by the United States it is a crime. The General Laws of Colorado provide: "All marriages between Negroes and mulattoes of either sex and white persons are declared absolutely void.... provided that nothing in this section shall be construed as to prevent the people living in that portion of the State acquired frum Mexico from marrying according to the custom of that country." The penalty is: "fine of not less than fifty nor more than five hundred dollars, or imprisonment for not less than three months, nor more than two years, or both, at the discretion of the court." (Chapter 63, 1736, Sec. 2 and 1737, Sec. 3. (1877).

IV. Phoebe Fraunces. She was the daughter of "Black Sam" Fraunces, a West Indian Negro at whose tavern in New York City, Washington and his officers used to eat, and where most of their revolutionary plans were discussed. In 1776, the British, hoping to head off the Revolution, tried to poison Washington. Their agent was Thomås Hickey, an Irishman, who had won Washington's confidence, and had been made his bodyguard. Hickey began by winning Phoebe's heart, then gave Phoebe, who used to wait on Washington, a dish of poisoned peas to serve him. Phoebe, despite her love for Hickey, warned Washington, who threw the peas into the yard. Chickens, there, picked them up and fell dead. Hickey was hanged before a crowd of 20,000 in New York City.

Had Washington, the soul of the Revolution, died then, America might not have been free.

M. E. Peirce says, "For this measureless service should not Phoebe some day have a tablet on the wall of her father's tavern?"—The Landmark of Fraunces Tavern, p. 21, 1901.

Wm. Hornor, Jr. in a well-documented article on Sam Fraunces in the Philadelphia Bulletin, Feb. 22, 1934, p. 8c, calls him "this fastidious old Negro," and says that he wore a wig over his curly hair. New York City: Guide Series, p. 68, (1939) says he was "a West Indian of French and Negro blood." See also article by Frederic J. Haskin, Washington, D. C. Evening Star, Aug. 11, 1916, p. 10.

Sam Fraunces was thanked by Congress for his services and given a sum of money. When Washington became president, Fraunces became steward of his household.

See also B. J. Lossing's Washington, Vol. I, Pt. 2, p. 176, 1859. 2 vols.

V. On May 9, 1862, Gen. Hunter of the Union Army issued a proclamation freeing the slaves of Georgia, Florida, and South Carolina, which Lincoln annulled. Lincoln said, "Gen. Hunter is an honest man....He proclaimed all men free within certain states. I repudiated the proclamation." (Complete Works of Abraham Lincoln, Vol. II, pp. 155, 205. New York, 1920.)

VI. Hannibal Hamlin, Civil War Vice-President, native of Maine, was strongly objected to by the South and its sympathizers, who declared he was a Negro. Once when attacked on the floor of Congress because of this, he retorted, "I take my complexion from nature. He gets his from the brandy bottle. Which is more honorable?—C. M. Hamlin, "Hannibal Hamlin," pp. 56, 354-56, Cambridge, 1899; J. R. Ficklen, History of Reconstruction in Louisiana, p. 30, Baltimore, 1911; Dict. of American Biography, Vol. VIII, p. 197; J. B. McMaster's History of the People of the United States, Vol. VIII, p. 484 N. Y. 1913.

VII. As first passed by Congress in 1861 and signed by President Buchanan, the thirteenth amendment was designed to make slavery perpetual by making it a states' right. Three Northern states ratified it at once but by this time the South wanted more than slavery: it wanted independence. Moreover, Lincoln and the anti-slavery party was soon afterwards in power. But as late as 1864, the Democrats in Congress still tried to win the South by offering it a free hand with slavery. General Gordon, Confederate leader, declared that had the South been content with slavery alone, there would have been no war.—Annual Report, 1896, American Historical Assn. (H. V. Ames), Vol. II, pp. 192-96.

1. In New York there are 375,999 illiterates in a white population of 10,513,933 or 3.6 per cent. Negro illiterates are 8,604 in a population of 347,381 or 2.5 per cent. (1930 Census, Vol. II, p. 1229).

2. See: The Negro Year Book, 1931-32, p. 166. Tuskegee Institute.

3. Some say that the word is from the Arabic, ka-wah; others, from "Caffa." The latter is clearly more plausible. Besides, at its introduction into England it was called, "caffe," "coffa," and "coffi." Capt. John Smith in his "Travels and Adventures" says "coffa," (1603). Francis Bacon, "coffe."

The Encyclopedia Brittanica says, "The use of coffee in Abyssinia was first recorded in the 15th Century, and was then stated to have been practised from time immemorial. Neighboring countries, however, appear to have been quite ignorant of its value." Vol. V, p. 973, 1936.

R. H. Hewitt says, "It derived its name from Kaffa, East Africa, where the plant also grows wild." (Coffee, p. 15, New York, 1872.)

In Abyssinia the coffee-merchants told me that the word originated from "Caffa."

Coffee has played a very important role in the political and literary destiny of mankind. Consult also W. H. Ukers; All About Coffee, pp. 5, 36. Also M. Gruhl, Citadel of Ethiopia, pp. 171-2.

4. Washington wrote Capt. Joh. Thompson from Mt. Vernon, July 2, 1776—"Sir: With this letter comes a Negro (Tom) which I beg the favor of you to sell in any of the islands you may go to for whatever he will fetch and bring me in return from him:

"One hhd. of best molasses
One ditto of best rum etc., etc."

(George Washington, Writings of, Vol. II, p. 211, N. Y.. 1889.)

5. The full quotation reads: "A certain loathsome disease which decimates the North American Indians and threatens extirpation to the South Sea Islanders dies out in the interior of Africa without the aid of medicine, and the Bangwaketse, who brought it from the West Coast lost it when they came into their own lands south of Klobeng. It seems incapable of permanence in any form in persons of pure African blood anywhere in the centre of the country; and the virulence of the secondary symptoms to be in all the cases that came under my care in exact proportion to the greater or less amount of European blood in the patient." (Missionary Travels and Researches in South Africa, p. 142, New York, 1858.)

Dr. T. D. Coleman said, "Tuberculosis was almost unknown to the Negro in his savage state." (A. Klebs: Tuberculosis, p. 118, New York, 1909.)

THE ARTS

6. In a reconstruction of Grimaldis by Alfred Rutot, a Grimaldi Negro artist is shown holding the Venus of Willendorf. (For reproductions of them see, Crisis Magazine, Feb. 1920: Dr. Frances Hoggan: Prehistoric Negroids and Their Contribution to Civilization, pub. in New York.)

E. Faure says: "The Venus of Willendorf, the most ancient human form in sculpture that we know." History of Art, Vol. I, page 13, (N. Y. 1931).

Dr. Verneau says, "The Grimaldi race is clearly a Negro one. The skeletons of the two Negroes of the Grotte des Enfants are complete and in a state of preservation which permits the describing of their characteristics with certitude." (L'Homme, Race, et Coutumes, pp. 24-37, Paris, 1931.)

Prof. E. Pittard of the University of Geneva, Switzerland, gives abundant support to Verneau in "Les Races et L'Histoire," pp. 81-86, Paris, 1924.

Histoire Universelle speaks of "Austria being inhabited by Negroes in the Paleolithic Age." (Vol. I, p. 55.)

G. F. Elliott says: "Whoever they (the Grimaldi) were their grave goods were the wealthiest and richest of their day and generation." (Prehistoric Man And His Story, p. 162.) Drawings strikingly like those in the caverns of Southern France, Spain, and Palestine have been found in South and East Africa. See also C. Van Riet Lowe; Illustrated London News, p. 606, April 29, 1933. F. Hertz: Race and Civilization, p. 101.

The late Prof. R. B. Dixon of Harvard University says that the presence of the Negro in Paleolithic times "has been universally admitted on the northern Mediterranean coast....It continued to be a clearly discernible factor in the population of Western Russia until the Middle Ages—Racial History of Mankind, p. 478. N. Y. 1923.

Griffith Taylor says, "Next in order in Europe would seem to be the Negrito race, of which more evidence is accumulating every year....We may label the fourth stratum, Negroid. These people must have been quite abundant in Europe towards the close of the Paleolithic....skulls of East Brazil show where similar folk penetrated to the New World."—Environment and Race, pp. 222-3. Lond. 1927.

The explorers, Neuville and Stekelis, discovered in a cave at Umm Qualifa at Wady Khareitum in Palestine, similar prehistoric drawings of elephants, rhinoceri, and other African animals. (London Times, October 6, 1932).

7. See 6.

8. Frederick Hertz, German anthropologist, in "Race and Civilization," refers twice to Beethoven's "Negroid traits" and his "dark" skin, and "flat, thick nose." (pp. 123 and 178.)

Frau Fischer, an intimate acquaintance of Beethoven, describes him thus, "Short, stocky, broad shoulders, short neck, round nose, blackish-brown complexion." (From R. H. Schauffler, The Man Who Freed Music, Vol. I, p. 18, 1929.)

In speaking of the immortal Haydn who was Beethoven's teacher, Andre de Hevesy, says: "Everybody knows the incident at Kismarton or Eisenstadt, the residence of Prince Esterhazy. In the middle of the first allegro of Haydn's symphony, His Highness asked the name of the author. He was brought forward.

"'What!' exclaimed the prince, 'the music is by this blackamoor? 'Well, my fine blackamoor, henceforward, thou art in my service.'"

Carpani, who originally related this says that "Haydn's complexion gave room for the sarcasm." And that Haydn had the title of "second professor of music but his new comrades called him The Moor." (G. Carpani: Le Haydine, etc. Letter 5. Milan, 1812.)

Referring to the above incident, Alexander W. Thayer, perhaps the foremost authority on Beethoven, says, "Beethoven had even more of the Moor in his features than his master, 'Haydn.'" (Beethoven, Vol. I, p. 146.) By "Moor" was meant "Negro." Until recent times the German for "Negro" was "Mohr."

Paul Bekker, another very noted authority on Beethoven, says that "the most faithful picture of Beethoven's head" shows him with "wide, thick-lipped mouth, short, thick nose, and proudly arched forehead." (Beethoven, p. 41, 1925. trans. Bozman). Thayer adds that Beethoven was an ugly, little man, and no one would be more astonished than the great composer should he return and see how he has been idealized by sculptors and painters.

Beethoven's family originated in Belgium, which had been ruled for centuries by the Spaniards, who had large numbers of Negro soldiers in their army there. Theophile Gautier speaks of a Belgian type characterized by brown skin and dark hair "a second race which the soldiers of the Spanish Duke of Alva have sown between Brussels and Cambrai."

In short, the general description of Beethoven, even to his frizzly hair, fits that of many an Aframerican or West Indian mulatto. In the Southern States Beethoven would have been forced to ride in the jim-crow car.

See also: Rogers, J. A., "Sex and Race," Vol. I, pp. 288, 289, 302 (1941) for other data on Beethoven's Negro strain, one of which is from the New York Times. Also p. 8 for portrait of Beethoven drawn from life by Hofel, which clearly shows the Negro strain. For more extended proof as well as a picture of Beethoven's life-mask see Sex and Race, Vol. 3, pp. 306-309.

9. See N. Leon: El Negrito Poeta Mexicano, Mexico City, 1912.

10. See 6.

ANCIENT CIVILIZATIONS

11. Persia was originally dominated by a Negro people known as the Elamites. Dieulafoy, a Frenchman, the principal excavator of Susa, the ancient Negro capital, says: "I shall attempt to show to what distant antiquity remounts the establishment of the Negroes upon the left bank of the Tigris and the constitution of the Susian monarchy....

"Towards 2300 B. C. the plans of the Tigris and Anzian Susinka were ruled by a dynasty of Negro kings.

"The coming of this dynasty of Medes corresponds perhaps to the arrival in the South of an immense Scythian (white) invasion.

"Pushed back by the black Susians, after having taken possession of the mountains the whites poured down upon the plans of Tigris and remained master of the country until the time when Kadur Nakunta subdued Chaldea and founded Anzan-Susinka, and who added to the territory of the blacks—Nime, Kussu, Habardip—all the mountainous districts inhabited by the whites of the Scythian race." (L'Acropole de Suse, pp. 27, 46, 102-115, Paris, 1893.)

That is to say, Chaldea, the land from which Abraham came, was conquered by these Negroes.

Dieulafoy adds: "The Greeks themselves seemed to have known these two Susian races. Have not their old poets given to the direct descendants of Memnon, the legendary Susian hero, who perished under the walls of Troy, a Negro father, Tithon, and a white mountain woman mother, Kissia? Do they not say that Memnon commanded an army of black and white regiments at the siege of Troy?" (p. 44).

Later the Aryans and the Susians united to form the Persian race. According to Eschylus, greatest poet of antiquity after Homer, Perses, the ancestor of the Persian people was the grandson of Epaphos, who was black like his father, Zeus. The great Persian rulers, Cyrus, Darius, Xerxes might have been mulattoes. The Negroes also conquered Assyria and Babylonia, under their leaders Shishak and Tirhaquah or Taharka, both of whom are mentioned in the Bible. Some of the Phoenician rulers as Tabnit and his famous son, Eshmunuzar II, were pure Negroes as their portraits in the

Louvre show. Whatever the Aryans might have been at first they were later, say, about 1100 B. C., very much mixed with the Negroes not only in Mesopotamia but in India. The term, Aryan, when used as a symbol of race purity by Hitler and others is the kind of idiocy that lunatics "tongue and brain not."

For further reference to these Negro peoples who ruled in Persia see: J. De Morgan: Mission Scientifique en Perse—Recherches Archael. Vol. IV, pp. 182-83. Paris, 1896. P. Sykes, Hist. of Persia, Vol. I, p. 51. G. Maspero: Hist. of Egypt, Vol. IV, pp. 41-55, which has pictures of the Susians.

12. The portrait of Cheops shows his Negro strain. See reproduction in Flinders Petrie: Abydos, Pl. XIV, Pt. II. London, 1903.

In the Ethiopian hall of the old Boston museum, I saw in 1924 a bust with the inscription, "Negro princess of the Cheops family." The new museum there has two limestone busts, one of a Negro prince, and the other a Negro princess of this family. See also G. H. Beardsley, The Negro in Greek and Roman Civilization, p. 12, Baltimore, 1929.

The testimony of eye-witnesses as well as that of modern science is that the Egyptians were Negroid, that is to say, largely mulatto, and the Ethiopians, unmixed Negroes.

Herodotus, (484-425 B. C.) very distinctly says that the Egyptians had black skins and woolly hair. (See No. 47.)

Aristotle, who was born 324 B. C. and still ranks as a great scientist clearly says too that the Egyptians were "very black" and the Ethiopians, "woolly-haired." (Physiognomy, Chap. VI.)

13. Herodotus says of his visit to Egypt, "The priests afterwards recited to me from a book the names of 330 sovereigns (successors of Menes); in this continued series eighteen were Ethiopians." (Book II, 100.)

For the conquest of Egypt by Piankhi see: J. H. Breasted: Ancient Records of Egypt, Vol. IV, p. 406-44, and Arthur Weigall: Exploits of the Nigger King in (Personalities of Antiquity). New York, 1928.

14. "But of all (the kings of Ethiopia) Ganges was most famous, who with his Ethiopian army passed into Asia and conquered all as far as the River Ganges, to which he left that name, being before called Chliaros." (Purchas: His Pilgrimage, Book VII, Africa, p. 551).

15. L. J. Morie traces the ancestry of the Ethiopian kings to "Cush.... born black in 6280 B. C." (Histoire de l'Ethiope, Vol. I, p. 207. Paris, 1904.)

"The Ethiopians list their kings from Ori of 4478 B. C. to Haile Selassie the First of A. D. 1930." (Nat. Geographic Maga, p. 683, June, 1931).

16. On the presence of the Negro in America before Columbus, C. C. Marquez, says, "The Negro type is seen in the most ancient Mexican sculpture....The Negroes figure frequently in the most remote traditions of some American pueblos....It is to this race doubtlessly belongs the most ancient skeletons of very distant structure of two of the Red American races which have been found in various places from Bolivia to Mexico." (Estudios Arqueoligicos y Etnograficos, pp. 270-73, Madrid, 1920). See also Prof. R. B. Dixon: Racial History of Mankind, pp. 400, 401, 409, 441, 449. Dixon emphasizes the fact that there was an early Negro strain in the Rhode Island, Massachusetts, and Central American Indians.

Columbus says, "He wanted to find out what the Indians had told him that there had come to it from the south and southeast Negro peoples." (Journal of the Third Voyage, p. 6.)

Peter Martyr, the amanuensis of Columbus, tells of Negroes living in Central America before the introduction of slavery and says, "These were the first Negroes seen in the Indies," (Descubrimiento de la Mar del Sur, in Lord Kingborough's Antiquities of Mexico, Vol. VI, p. 291.)

Prof. Leo Weiner of Harvard University says, "The presence of Negroes with their trading masters before Columbus is proved by the representation of Negroes in American sculpture and design; by the occurrence of a black nation at Darien early in the 16th Century, but more specifically by Columbus' emphatic reference to Negro traders from Guinea....The chief cultural influence was exerted by a Negro colony in Mexico." (Africa and the Discovery of America, Vol. III, pp. 365-369, Philadelphia, 1920-2.)

Colonel A. Braghine says that he saw in Ecuador a statuette of a Negro that is at least "20,000 years old." He adds, "Hitherto the ethnologists imagined that Negroes appeared in the New World only during our own epoch when they were imported as slaves . . . . Some statues of the Indian gods in Central America possess typical Negro features and certain prehistoric monuments there undoubtedly represent Negroes . . . ." (The Shadow of Atlantis, pp 40-42. N. Y. 1940.)

V. Riva Palacio says, "It is indisputable that in very ancient times.... the Negro raee occupied our territory (Mexico) when the two continents were joined. This race brought its own religious cults and ideals. (Mexico a traves de los siglos, vol. I, pp. 63-67. Mexico, 1887.) "The Mexicans recall a Negro god, Ixtlilton, which means black-faced." p. 163.

17. One of the principal reasons for this theory, as Delafosse says, is "all the Negro tribes of Africa assert that their first ancestors came from the East." (M. Delafosse: Les Noirs de l'Afrique, p. 6, Paris.) There is a translation of this work by F. Fliegelman, Washington, D. C. 1931.

This was true even of Ancient Egypt. The celebrated Negro Queen of Egypt, Hatshepsut, sent an expedition eastwardly to Punt in Arabia, from which land the Egyptians believed their ancestors came.

Of the Bushmen, the Hottentots, and other original Negroid natives of Africa, the Catholic Encyclopedia says, "Traces of a similar population are found in Europe and at the present day a parallel race is represented by the Negritos of the Andamans, Moluccas, and the islands of the vicinity of Indo-China. These little men would therefore seem to have occupied the whole of the ancient continent (Africa)....they look on themselves and are looked on by their neighbors as the first owners of the Earth." (Vol. I, p. 182.)

Sir H. H. Johnston, one of the foremost authorities on the Negro, says, "The deductions....point rather to India as the original birthplace of the Negro." (Negro in the New World, pp. 24-27, London, 1910.)

See also: H. J. Peake: Early Steps in Human Progress, p, 23, London, 1933. J. F. Rock's discovery of the Chinese Negroes is mentioned in the New York Times, Nov. 26, 1933. E. W. P. Chinnery and his discovery of New Guinea Negroes, N. Y. Times, Sept. 16, 1934.

18. The wording of this is from the Provost-Marshal General's Office. Second Report on the Operations of the Selective Service System to Dec. 20, 1918, p. 193, pub. 1919.

ILLITERACY AND INTELLIGENCE

19. The illiteracy percentage of the following European countries as estimated by the U. S. Bureau of Education is:

Servia, 48 per cent, Bulgaria 55; Portugal, 60-70 per cent; Hungary, 10-20; Finland, Lithuania, Poland, 30-40; Rumania and Spain, 40-50; Italy, 20-30; Russia, 50-60. "Greece," says the report, "is considerably in excess of 50 per cent." "Spain, Italy and Bulgaria show comparatively high rates."

(Illiteracy in the Several Countries of the World," Bulletin, 1929, No. 4. Dept. of the Interior.)

These figures are largely for 1920, when Aframerican illiteracy was 22.9. The latter is now 16.3.

Sixty-two per cent of the world's population can neither read nor write.

20. Negro illiteracy in California is 3.1 per cent; Minnesota: 2.0; New York: 2.5; Nevada: 1.5; South Dakota: 2.2; Oregon: 2.5; Washington: 2.9. The illiteracy of the Native American Whites of White parentage is, Virginia: 5.0; West Virginia: 3.8; North Carolina: 5.7; South Carolina: 5.2; Georgia: 3.4; Kentucky: 5.9; Tennessee: 5.4; Alabama: 4.9; Arkansas: 3.5; Louisiana: 7.8; and New Mexico: 8.2 (U. S. Census, Vol. II, p. 1229.)

21. See American Journal of Sociology, Vol. 33, p. 256 (Sept. 1927).

22. The quotation is from J. Dietz' Autobiography, p. 68, translated by Bernard Miall, first published by Dr. E. Consentius, N. Y., 1923. See also p. 290.

With regard to cannibalism in Germany, Hertz says, "The Thirty Years' War (1618-48) brought such dire misery to Germany that Cannibalism began to rear its ghastly head as is attested by the minutes of the town council of Ruffach in 1636. Duke Charles of Lorraine maintained that his soldiers once roasted children in order to eat them and that they once boiled two old nuns for the sake of having good strong broth. Borneman reported in 1639 'that two children devoured their dear mother after she had died from starvation and Lord, have mercy on us, acts of this kind occur daily here. A certain bailiff, Schulte, reported in 1643 that men were being caught in snares and regularly roasted." (Race and Civilization, p. 256.)

The Ethiopians of that time also used to make mumia from their captives and criminals. (Purchas His Pilgrimage, p. 616. London, 1613.)

EXPLORATION

23. J. K. Hosmer says of the first journey made across the American continent by civilized men, "Of these, three were Spaniards, and the fourth, a person upon whom it is worth while to dwell for a moment. He was a Negro, the first of his race to reach the valley, contemporary with the earliest Europeans." Of Estevanico's expedition to Arizona and New Mexico, he says, "Fray Marcos sent the Negro forward as better fitted than anyone to prepare the way." (A Short History of the Mississippi Valley pp. 25-27, Boston, 1901.)

For the account of the actual journey see: Narrative of Nunez Cabeca de Vaca, N. Y. 1922. Also J. E. Bolton: Chronicles of America, Vol. 23.

24. See Wisconsin Historical Collections, Vol. 23. Mission Fields at Home, March, 1934. An exhibit at the Chicago Fair (1933-34) featured Bapsiste Pointe de Saible as the first settler of that city. R. Shackleton says, "The first settler of Chicago as distinguished from explorers and temporary abiders, was, as Chicagoans, themselves, express it, a black man . . . a West Indian Negro." (p. 14. 1920).

25. Heinrich Brode: Life of Tippo Tib, London, 1907. Alfred Swann: Fighting the Slave Hunters, pp. 75, 86, 171-75, London, 1910.

26. Consult M. Henson's own account: A Negro at the North Pole. New York, 1912. Hampton's Magazine, Jan. 1910. Liberty Magazine, July 17, 1926. Henson dragged Peary to the North Pole, and while the latter was asleep Henson walked ahead and stood at the Pole before any other member of the expedition.

SCIENCE AND INVENTION

27. Marcosson says, "A Dutch Guiana Negro, who worked in one of the Lynn shops, had invented a somewhat crude machine to last shoes which saved much time and labor. After the usual fashion of inventors he had hawked it about with no success. Winslow heard of it and together with Geo. W. Brown....bought and backed this patent, which became the nucleus of the great United Shoe Manufacturing Company. These two men now dominate the concern, which produces 300 machines for making shoes and employs more than 5000 people. The Millionaire Yield of Boston in Munsey Magazine, August, 1912, (p. 723). Also F. A. Gannon: History of American Shoe-Making.

Waldemar Kaempffert says of him, "A poor half-breed son of a Dutch engineer and a native black woman. This messenger from a foreign land solved the final problem in making shoes by machinery."—Popular History of American Invention, Vol. II, pp. 429-30, N. Y. 1924.

Naturally attempts have been made to prove that Matzeliger was white. His death certificate, however, recorded him as a mulatto, a fact which his portrait ensures. For a photograph of the invention see, C. G. Woodson's The Negro In Our History.

28. "Thomas Edison, the world's greatest inventor, sent his personal representative to Tuskegee for the purpose of making Dr. Carver join his mighty forces at Orange Grove, N. J." (A. H. Merritt: From Captivity to Fame, p. 38, Boston, 1929.)

JEWS AND ETHIOPIANS

29. The Koran reads: "And he (Moses) drew forth his hand out of his bosom and behold it appeared white unto the spectators." (Chap. vii, p. 128.) "And put thy right hand under thy left arm; it shall come forth white." (Sale: Al Koran, p. 257. 1784.)

Sale adds: "There is a tradition that Moses was a very swarthy man." (p. 128.)

Sir T. W. Arnold says, "According to Mohammedan tradition, Moses was a black man." (The Preaching of Islam, p. 106. Westminster, 1896.)

The Vulgate and the modern Bible say that Moses' hand was "leprous as snow," but the Septuagint Bible, which is the oldest translation, dating to about 150 B. C., accords with the Koran. The Septuagint says that Moses' hand "became as snow," and that when he placed it in his bosom the second time "it was restored to the complexion of the other flesh." (Exod. IV. 6.) Here is the clearest possible inference that the miracle lay in turning a black skin, white, and then changing it to black again. I have similar references on this subject.

The argument so often made that Miriam's objection to Moses' Ethiopian wife was one of color, is wrong. There was no color prejudice then. Besides the Jews at that time were also colored. Miriam's objection must have been a national or tribal one, the same as exists among the Negroes on the West African coast now, and among the Jews themselves in India.

30. Tacitus says: "Many again say that they (the Jews) were a race of Ethiopian origin." (Book V, Chap. 2.)

F. Ratzel says: "The entire Semitic and Hamitic population of Africa was a mulatto character which extends to the Semites outside of Africa." (History of Mankind, Vol. II, p. 246.)

M. Fishberg, a leading Jewish authority, says: "Contrary to generally accepted theory that they (the Jews) have maintained their racial purity for centuries research by modern anthropological methods has shown that the physical type of the Jews bears a striking resemblance to the ethnic types encountered in indigenous races and peoples among whom they happen to live." (North African Jews, p. 1, New York, 1906.) That is to say that in the black man's land the Jew is black; in the brown man's land, brown; and in the white man's land, white, etc. Fishberg gives abundant illustration of this by pictures. For the Negro Jew, see his book, "The Jew," pp. 120-134, 146, 149, 174, 178, 181. F. Hertz says: "In China, the Jews are hardly to be distinguished from the Chinese; in Africa they look like the Negro...."

Abraham came from Ur of the Chaldees (Gen. 11, 31.) Godfrey Higgins, a careful and reliable English antiquary, says. "The Chaldees were originally Negroes." (Anacalypsis, Vol. II, p. 364. New York, 1927.)

For the number of Jews, who entered and left Egypt, see, Gen. 46:27, and Exod., 12:37. For the number of years in Egypt: Exod. 12:40.

As regards the Negro origin of the Jew, Count Adam Gurowski, of Poland, says, "Numbers of Jews have the greatest resemblance to the American mulattoes. Sallow carnation complexion, thick lips, crisped black hair. Of all the Jewish population scattered over the globe one-fourth dwells in Poland. I am therefore well acquainted with their features. On my arrival in this country (the United States) I took every light-colored mulatto for a Jew."—America and Europe, p. 117, N. Y., 1857.

Sir H. H. Johnston attributes much of the prejudice against the Jew to the latter's Negro origin. He says: "In the Jew, as in the Egyptian and the Moor, there is a varying but still discernible element of the Negro, derived in the case of the Jew from the strong infusion of Elamite blood and in the case of the Moor from the obvious connection with the Negro...." (World Position of the Negro and Negroid, in G. Spiller: Universal Races Congress, p. 330, London, 1911.) But this viewpoint is wrong. There is very little or no prejudice against the Negro in Europe, outside of England. In Vienna the darkest Negroes are welcomed in places from which the fairest Jew is barred. Moreover, this opposition against the Jew is to be found even in the black and the brown men's lands. Algeria was recently the scene of much anti-Jewish rioting.

For the classing together of Jew and Ethiopian, see Amos, 9:7.

For a discussion at length of the Egyptian and Ethiopian origin of the Jews, see: Gerald Massey: A Book of the Beginnings, Vol. II, pt. 2, pp. 364-441, London, 1881. See also Chapter, "Were the Jews Originally Negroes," pp. 91-95, in Sex and Race, Vol. I, 1941.

31. Fishberg says of the Falasha Jews: "They are of the Negro type.... the large lips, the prognathism, and frizzly hair, all point to the Negro origin." (The Jew, p. 147.) I have seen the Falashas in Abyssinia and the Negro Jews in Egypt and the Sudan. West Africa has black Jews also.

H. Norden says of these Abyssinian Jews, "My stay among them carried something of the quality of interest and excitement of the imagination with the sight of things excavated after centuries of burial. It formed a bridge from the present to the past. Biblical chronicles were no longer to me merely ancient religious history. They became the records of the life of a people not unlike the Falashas." (Chap. "Among the Black Jews" in "Africa's Last Empire," p. 203.)

Whilst in Ethiopia I visited the Falasha school established by Dr. Faitlovitch. The boys were all jet-black with woolly hair.

For the Jewish conquest of Abyssinia see L. J. Morie: Histoire de L'Ethiope, Vol. II, p. 181-83, Paris, 1904; and African Society Jour., Vol. 28, p. 60.

32. The Black Jews of India "are kept at a respectable distance and not permitted to enter the synagogues of the whites nor do they bury their dead in the same cemetery." (M. Fishberg: The Jew, p. 134; Isaac, I. A. Cochin Jews, 1917.)

MEDICINE

33. Gerald Massey says of Imhotep, "The child-Christ remained a starrily-bejewelled blackamoor as the typical healer in Rome. Jesus the divine healer, does not retain the black complexion of Iu-em-hotep (Imhotep) in the canonical Gospels, but he does in the Church of Rome when represented as a little black bambino. A jewelled image of the child-Christ as a blackamoor is sacredly preserved at the headquarters of the Franciscan order and true to its typical character as a symbolical likeness of Iusa, the healer, the little black figure is taken out in state with its regalia on to visit the sick and demonstrate the supposed healing power of this Egyptian, Esculapius, thus Christianized. The virgin mother who was also black survived in Italy as in Egypt. At Oropa near Bietta, the Madonna and her child-Christ are not white, but black as they so often were in Italy of old and as the child is yet conditioned in the little black Jesus of the Eternal City. Surely the profoundest sigh of an ever-warring world went up to heaven in the cult of Iu-em-hotep (Imhotep) who was worshipped as the giver of rest, the Kamite prince of peace." (Ancient Egypt: The Light of the World, Vol. II, p. 754, London, 1907.)

The statuettes of Imhotep in the Cairo Museum show his Negroid features. They are reproduced in G. Daressy's, Catalogue General des Antiquities Egyptiennes du Musee du Caire, Plate IV, 38,045 to 38,050, and Plate V.

34. "The Negro doctor, Aben Ali, attached to the suite of Charles VII had the glory of curing Charles whilst he was still Dauphin." (C. de la Ronciere: Negres et Negriers, p. 11, Paris, 1933.)

35. Information on Dr. Tavares was received personally by me from Senhor Mario Domingues, prominent Portuguese writer, whose address article by de Lara on Dr. Tavares, together with his portrait in "Africa Magazine," Lisbon, April, 1932.

36. Medical Record, March 27, 1897. The patient was James Cornish. Dr. Williams lived in Chicago. I knew him personally for many years.

POLITICS

37. J. B. Clarke mentions Heredia, who was a Cuban, as Minister in the Rouvier Cabinet in 1887, in "A Momento of The Emancipation Proclamation Exposition of New York State, 1913," p. 23. See also L'Abolition de l'Esclavage au Bresil," which is the proceedings of a banquet held in Paris, July 10, 1888, to commemorate the abolition of slavery in Brazil, where Heredia was a guest.

Diagne's appointment as Cabinet Minister was widely heralded. See N. Y. Times, Jan. 27, 1931. For the appointment of Delmont and Candace, consult French papers of the period. I was present at each of the banquets given in honor of the last-named three. I have met all, save Heredia.

Senator Henry Lemery was in the Clemenceau Cabinet, and was Minister of Justice in the Doumergue Cabinet.

Candace as late as 1939 was vice-president of the Chamber of Deputies and head of the budget for the French Navy.

38. Vincent Sheean says in part of Eugene Chen, "The Foreign Minister was a remarkable man....Physically and in some ways of speech, Mr. Chen reminded me of the French politician, Malvy; his complacency was like that of Austen Chamberlain; his delight in his own language and the care that he took to see that it was written down in its baroque magnificence suggested Mussolini. He was theatrical as Briand without any of the old fox's charm; he was an ingratiating as Streseman, as bitter as Poincare. In short Mr. Chen was a politician....Mr. Chen had been born a British subject at Trinidad, West Indies. His name as a British subject was not Chen. He was of mixed race, part Chinese, part Negro....He had chosen his wife from the Negro race, and in his four charming children the Chinese strain seemed almost to have vanished." Personal History, pp. 205-07, N. Y., 1935. John Gunther, "Inside Asia," pp. 259-60, 264, 269, New York, 1939. Chen's real name was Akam.

RACE-MIXING

39. Persina, in her defense, says to her mulatto daughter, "Thou wert born white which color is strange among the Ethiopians: I knew the reason because I looked upon the picture of Andromeda naked while my husband had to do with me....yet I determined to rid myself of shameful death counting it certain that the color would procure me to be accused of adultery." (Ethiopian History of Heliodorus—Underwood 1597—Book IV, p. 102.) This story is a romance with a probable basis of fact.

Regarding Louise-Marie, the mulatto daughter of Maria Theresa, Queen of France, there is indisputable record of her birth in the diary of Mademoiselle de Montpensier, the King's first cousin. She says, "The child that the Queen had just given birth to resembled the little dwarf that M. de Beaufort had brought from a foreign country; that he was well-formed in his race of dwarf and Negro; and that the child did not seem that it would live." (Memoires de Mlle. de Montpensier, Tome V, pp. 118-19, Paris, 1728.)

The Duke de St. Simon says: "It is said that she was the daughter of the King and the Queen, that her color had caused her to be hidden there, and after her disappearance, to be published that the Queen had a miscarriage. Many of the people of the court believe this. But whatever it be it remains a mystery." (Memoires, Vol. I, p. 258, years 1697-98.)

Voltaire declared that he visited the convent where this girl was imprisoned and that he saw her. Her picture hangs now in the Library of St. Genevieve, Paris, France. It represents a Negro woman with bright eyes, a long, fleshy nose, thick lips and a long face. The documents concerning her disappeared mysteriously. Today only the cover for them remains. But it bears the title, "The Princess Louise-Marie, daughter of Louis XIV and Maria-Theresa." Victor Hugo believed that the Negro was the father of Louise-Marie.

The writer who said that the color of the child was due to the mother's fondness for chocolate was La Marquise de Sevigne. Maria Theresa ate so much chocolate that it blackened her teeth. But it was not to the Queen that La Marquise de Sevigne referred. It was to another noble lady, who had a similar accident. "The Marquise de Coetlogen," says Mme. de Sevigne, "ate so much chocolate, being big with child, that last year she gave birth to a little boy, black as the devil." (Lettres de Mme. de Sevigne, Oct. 25, 1671, Vol. III, p. 10, Paris, 1818.)

The noble ladies of France, Germany and England had coal-black pages about them "to set off the whiteness of their skin." They, too, seemed to have been very fond of "chocolate." The same was true of the American ladies in slavery days. It is a well-known fact in Chicago that the daughter of that city's once leading millionaire eloped with a "chocolate."

40. Anna, the Negro concubine of Pope Clement VII, is mentioned by C. W. King in speaking of the Negro vogue in jewels that prevailed in the sixteenth century. He says, "The same age was a little later extremely fruitful in heads of Negroes and Negresses, the latter often in the character of Cleopatra holding to her breast the asp. There is reason to believe that some of the latter are intended to commemorate the renowned black concubine of Clement VII, the mother of Alessandro dei Medici." (Antique Rings and Gems, p. 326, London, 1872.)

Consult also Gino Capponi: Storia della Repubblica di Firenze, Vol. III, p. 167, Florence, 1871; Nuova Enciclopedia Italiana, Vol. 13, p. 1035. Torino, 1882; G. F. Young: The Medici, Vol. I, p. 439, London, 1909. All three says that Anna was a mulatto.

41. In Sept. 1664, Maryland passed a law that any white woman who married a Negro should serve the master of such slave "for life." Slaveholders took advantage of this law to induce the white women, some of whom were recent arrivals, to marry the Negroes. MacCormac says, "Instead of preventing such marriages this law enabled avaricious and unprincipled masters to convert many of their (White) servants into slaves." In 1681, the Legislature was forced to issue the following law: "Divers freeborn English or White women sometimes by the instigation, procurement, and connivance of their masters....and always to the satisfaction of their lascivious and lustful desires....do intermarry with Negroes and other slaves, be it enacted that if any master....having any freeborn English or white woman servant in their possession or property, shall by any instigation, procurement, knowledge, permission or contrivance," cause her to marry a slave she should be free at once and the master should pay a fine of "10,000 lbs. of tobacco." (Archives of Maryland, Vol. I, pp. 433-34, and Vol. III, pp. 203-04, also Johns Hopkins University Studies in Hist. & Pol. Science, No. 3 & 4.) What is true of Maryland was true of other states.

42. Calhoun says, "A considerable proportion of Jefferson's slaves were his own children. If any of them made off he would smile as if to imply that he would not be urgent in pursuit. He bequeathed freedom to five of his children and the Assembly passed a law allowing them to remain in the state." (A. W. Calhoun: Social History of the American Family, Vol. II, p. 300, Cleveland, Ohio, 1918.

Jefferson's favorite concubine was the famous "Black Sal." The following are two lines from "The Jeffersoniad," written about both of them:

"Or seek in dark and dirty alley
A Mr. Jefferson's Miss Sally." (p. 7-16.)

Jefferson had Black Sal to take his white daughter to France—H. W. Pierson, Jefferson at Monticello, pp. 107-110. N. Y. 1862. At Jefferson's death-bed was an almost white Negro girl believed to be his daughter, but which the writer says belonged to another man, evidently noted, because he leaves the name blank, p. 110.

One of Jefferson's daughters was sold as a slave at New Orleans, see: Liberator, Vol. 8, p. 152, Sept. 21, 1838. For other sources see: Sex and Race, Vol. II, pp. 197, 221. 1942.

For Patrick Henry's Negro son, Melancthon, see: C. Fairbank: How The Way Was Prepared, p. 196, Chicago, 1890.

43. Napoleon said: "The question of the liberty of the blacks is very complicated and difficult (in Haiti). In Africa and Asia it has been resolved, but it has been so by means of polygamy. The whites and the blacks there form part of the same family. The head of the family having white and black wives and wives of color, the white and the mulatto children are brothers, are bred in the same cradle, bear the same name, and eat at the same table. Would it then be impossible to authorize polygamy in our islands, restricting the number of wives to two, one white, one black? The first Consul (Napoleon) had several conferences with the theologians on this grand measure." Historical Miscellanies, Vol. I, p. 217, London, 1823.)

44. Utting says: "They sailed in 1787 from Portsmouth with 60 white women whom the Government wished to exile; the latter were made drunk, carried on board, and married to the Negroes without their consent being asked." (F. A. J. Utting: Sierra Leone, p. 81, London, 1931.)

Mrs. A. M. Falconbridge, who talked with these women in Sierra Leone says that they "were mostly of that description of persons who walk the streets of London and support themselves by the earnings of prostitution; that men were employed to collect and conduct them to Wapping where they were intoxicated with liquor, then inveigled on board ship and married to Black men whom they had never seen before." (Voyages to Sierra Leone in 1791-2-3, pp. 64-66.)

45. Demaison says, "Mrs. Leybonn, who is of English origin, is the real queen of Rio Pongo. Although the other slave-traders are jealous of her commercially, she wields great influence over them. She has three mulatto children, a boy and two girls, who also engage in the slave-trade. One of the daughters has married Mr. Emerson, and the other Mr. Campbell, a British Consul at Lagos." (A. Demaison: Faidherbe, p. 273. Paris, 1932, 3rd ed.)

46. "The mulatto, some say, Negro, who married the Countess de Beauharnais, divorced, was named Castaing." (Intermediare des Chercheurs et des Curieux, Vol. 58, p. 582. Paris, 1893.) See also Duke de Pasquier, Memoirs, Vol. I, p. 128. Duchess d'Abrantes, Memoires, Vol. V.

RELIGION

47. Count C. F. Volney speaking of the mulatto appearance of the Egyptian people said, "but when I visited the Sphinix I could not help thinking the figure of that monster furnished the solution of the enigma, when I saw its features precisely those of a Negro. I recalled the remarkable passage of Herodotus in which he says, 'For my part I believe the Colchi to be a colony of Egyptians, because like them they have black skins and woolly hair,'—that is to say, the ancient Egyptians were real Negroes of the same species with all the natives of Africa." (Voyages en Syrie, etc., pp. 74-75, Paris, 1787.)

J. P. Widney says, "They (the Negroid races) once occupied a much wider territory and wielded a vastly greater influence upon earth than they do now. They are found chiefly in Africa, yet traces of them are to be found through the islands of Malaysia, remnants, no doubt of that more numerous black population which seems to have occupied tropical Asia before the days of the Semites, the Mongol, and the Brahminic Aryan." (Race Life of the Aryans, Vol. III, p. 238, New York, 1907.)

Schure, noted French writer on religion and mysticism, says, "The Blacks invaded Southern Europe in prehistoric times and were finally driven back by the Whites. Remembrances of them have disappeared from popular tradition. The Blacks, however, have left two ineffacable imprints in Europe: the horror of the dragon which was the emblem of their kings, and our idea that evil, or the devil is black. The Negroes returned the insult to the White race by making the devil, white. During the time of their sovereignty the Blacks had religious centres in Upper Egypt and in India. Their cyclopean cities embattled the mountains of Africa, the Caucasus, and Central Asia." (Edouard Schure: Les Grand Inities, p. 6, 113th edition. Paris, 1931.)

The statement of Father Fernandez is quoted from M. Russell: Nubia and Abyssinia, p. 275, New York, 1833.

48. Godfrey Higgins says, "We have found the black complexion or something relating to it whenever we have approached to the origin of nations. The Alma Mater, the Goddess Multimammia, the founders of the oracles, the Memnon or first idols were always black. Venus, Jupiter, Apollo, Bacchus, Hercules, Asteroth, Adonis, Horus, Apis, Osiris, Ammon—in short, all the wood and stone Deities were black. They remained as they were first made in very remote times." (Anacalypsis, Vol. I, p. 286.)

According to Sir E. A. W. Budge and others most of the earliest Egyptian gods as Ptah, "Father of the Gods" and Bes, god of war, mischief, and comedy, originated in the Sudan, the land of the Negroes. "From Fetish to God in Ancient Egypt," pp. 254-55, London, 1934.

The Greek gods were adaptations of the Egyptian ones, hence the earliest ones of Greece were also black. "Ethiop is a title of Zeus," says Higgins. Zeus was Father of the Gods among the Greeks.—The Celtic Druids, p. 162 (1829).

There is every indication that the earliest gods of both the Old and New World were Negroes.

As regards the Black Christ and Virgin, Romain Rolland, noted French writer, says, "Why are the majority of the Virgins that are revered in the celebrated pilgrimages, black? At Boulogne-sur-mer, the sailors still carry a Black Virgin in the procession. At Clermont in Auvergne, the Black Virgin is revered as also at Einsiendeln, Switzerland, near Zurich, to which thousands of pilgrims—Swiss, Bavarians, Alsatians—go to pay homage. The famous Virgin of Oropa in the Piedmont is still a Negro woman, as well as the not less legendary one at Montserrat in Catalonia, which receives 60,000 visitors a year. I have been able to trace the history of this one to the year 718 A.D., and it was always black. Tradition says that it was St. Luke who knew personally the Mother of Christ, and carved with his own hand, the majority of these Black Virgins. It is interesting to know, therefore, that if the Mother of Christ was not a Negro woman, how it happens that she is black in France, Switzerland, Italy, and Spain." Intermediare des Chercheurs et des Curieux, Vol. 34, p. 193.

Gerald Massey says, "The Black Jesus is a well-known form of the child-Christ worshipped on the Continent (European) where the black Bambino was the pet image of the Italian Church, as popular as Chrishna, the Black Christ of India, and unless the Divine Son was incarnated in black flesh from the....black Sut Nahsi, the Negro image of the earliest god....And finally the black Jesus of the Christian cult, the son of the Virgin Mother in the Romish Church." A Book of the Beginnings, Vol. 2, pt. 1, pp. 300, 340. London, 1881.

See also No. 33.

49. Quoted from J. H. Breasted, "The Dawn of Conscience," p. xv, New York, 1933. See also No. 30, in "100 Amazing Facts About the Negro," and same No. in "The Proof."

50. For a comparison of one of the Psalms of Akhenaton with the 104th Psalm in the Bible see Arthur Weigall: Life and Times of Akhenaton, pp. 134-136. New York, 1923. Also J. H. Breasted, History of Egypt, p. 373. New York, 1926.

51. The Ethiopian king in question was Shabaka, popularly called Sabacon, founder of the Ethiopian Dynasty, and conqueror of Assyria of whom Diodorus Siculus who travelled in Egypt 60 B. C. said, "Sabacon, an Ethiopian, came to the throne, going beyond all his predecessors in worship of the gods and in kindness to his subjects." Book I, Chap. V.)

The original document came from Ethiopia and was about 2,500 years older than the copy according to Breasted. He says, "Priceless are the mutiliated passages which still remain legible on this venerable block. We learn something of its origin at once from a line of stately hieroglyphics at the top where we find the name of the Ethiopian Pharaoh, who ruled Egypt in the Eighth Century, B. C.

"Following his name his inscription reads and states: 'His Majesty (meaning himself) wrote out this writing anew in the house of his father, Ptah-South-of-His-Wall. His Majesty had found it as a work of his ancestors." This pious Ethiopian King of Egypt was interested in preserving an ancient writing of his ancestors....

"The document (the original) is enormously old. We have mirrored in it the oldest thoughts of men that anywhere come down to us in written form." (The Dawn of Conscience, pp. 30-31, New York, 1933.) The slab is now in the British Museum. Sabacon was a brother of Pianki, Ethiopian conqueror of Egypt. (See No. 13.)

52. For African birth of the Popes, see Liber Pontificalis (Book of the Popes), p. 17, for Pope Victor; for Melchiades, sometimes called Miltiades, p. 40; for Gelasius, p. 110 (L. R. Loomis, translator. New York, 1916.) These Popes came from a region where the population was originally Negro, and is still Negroid. The whitest people in North Africa today are the Kabyles and of these Weisgerber says, "All the Kabyles of the Riff, of the Grand Kabylie, of the Aures, of the Enfida, belonging to the white Mediterranean race are more or less mixed with....Negroes." (Les Blancs d'Afrique, p. 83, Paris, 1910.) No color distinction has ever existed in North Africa hence the Negro strain, to a great degree, runs through the entire native population.

There are no authentic portraits of the earlier Popes. Such drawings of them as exist are all modelled to resemble that of St. Peter's, which like that of Christ, is apocryphal. There are real portraits of the Roman Emperors, however, and in that of Septimus Severus, who was an African, one can perceive Negroid traits.

On my second visit to the Catacombs of San Calixto with a party of colored people, the guide took us aside from the white tourists and showed us the tomb of Melchiades explaining that like us, he was African. Most of the leading fathers of the early Christian Church were Africans.

53. "Adoration" by Hans Baldung, German painter, shows St. Maurice as a very black Negro with the German-eagle on his head. For a reproduction, see H. Schmitz: Hans Baldung, p. 2, Leipsig, 1922.

For Hitler with the German eagle on his head, see: Illustrated London News, p. 651, May 6, 1933.

The most noted picture of St. Maurice is by Grunewald, in the Old Pinokathek, Munich. It represents a Negro of purest type. For reproduction, see: H. H. Josten: Matthias Grunewald, p. 81, Leipzig, 1921. Hitler's adopted emblem—the swastika—is perhaps the oldest known human symbol and is related to the cross which also is prehistoric. It was used by the black peoples of Africa and Polynesia thousands of years ago as well as by the American Indians. It is also the emblem of the Basques, a European people who are believed to be of African ancestry. In Bayonne, France, I saw a Basque shop with swastika ornaments and the sign "The Basques had the swastika 2500 years".

RULERS

54. Hannibal is usually depicted as a white man, but his coins in the British Museum and the Museo Kercheriano, Rome, show him to have been an African of purest type with rings in his ears. Col. Hennebert, perhaps the leading authority on Hannibal, declares that none of the several differing portraits now exhibited as Hannibal is he, "We do not possess any authentic portrait of Hannibal," he says. (Histoire d'Annibal, Vol. I, p. 495, Paris, 1870.) These coins were struck by Hannibal while he was in Italy. In the absence of other information the most logical argument is that they bore his own effigy, the more so, as the several kinds of them bear the same likeness. Above all, let us remember that he was an African.

55. Makkari says, "The first Sultan of the Almoravides, belongs to the tribe of the Masufuh. They inhabited the desert bordering upon the Sudan. (Mohammedan Dynasties in Spain, p. 386, Vol. I, London, 1840.)

Yusuf is called a Berber, but Westermarck says of the Berbers of this region, "There has been a Negro influence, which, among the Berbers of the South, no doubt commenced at a very early period when the southern border of their territory was more northerly than it is now and which has been maintained in later times through the influx of Negro slaves." (Ritual and Belief in Morocco, p. 12, London, 1926.)

The Encyclopedia Britannica says, "The Mohammedan princes of Andalusia (Spain) began to look to Africa where Yusuf-ben Tachfin was ruling the newly-founded empire of the Almoravides....Yusuf came and in 1086 inflicted a terrible defeat on Alphonso VI at Zalacca."

"The Almoravides....were Berbers and were largely mingled with pure Negroes...." (Vol. 21, p. 128, 14th edition.)

The "Rouad el-Kartas," a Moorish work, describes Yusuf as having a "brown colour....woolly hair."—Trans. by Beaumier, Histoire du Maghreb, p. 190.

The foremost Berber chief today is Prince Thami El-Glaoui, a dark mulatto. (See his portrait in my, "World's Greatest Men of African Descent." New York, 1931.)

56. See: F. Dubois: Timbuctoo the Mysterious. London, 1896. Abderrahman Es'Saadi: Tarik-es-Sudan. Paris, 1898.

57. Abraha Al-Ashram, an ex-slave, who rose to be emperor of Yemen and Ethiopia, went to the defense of the Yemenite Christians against the Jews in Arabia and attacked Mecca in 569 A. D. He was beaten back when his magnificent elephant, Mahmoud the Praiseworthy, knelt in the gate of the city, and refused to move. To the Mohammedans this event ranks second in importance only to the birth of Mohamet, who was born that year. This is known as "The Era of the Elephant," (see Chap. 105 of the Koran, or Mohammedan Bible), and it marks the beginning of the long conflict between Christianity and Mohammedanism. Later this struggle entered Europe, when Tarik invaded Spain in 711 A. D. The Christians retaliated with the Wars of the Crusades.

Abraha died soon after his defeat. Thirty-three years later the Ethiopians, who were the defenders of Christianity in the East, were driven back across the Red Sea. Gibbon, in his "Decline and Fall of the Roman Empire," says of this incident, "If a Christian power had been maintained in Arabia, Mohamet must have been crushed in his cradle and Abyssinia would have prevented a revolution which has changed the civil and religious state of the world."

For sketches of Abraha's life see: Biographie Universelle (Michaud), Vol. I, p. 89, W. B. Harris: Yemen, p. 317, and the Encyclopedia of Islam.

58. Abbe Dominique Busnot who was sent by Louis XIV to negotiate for the ransom of the white French slaves of Muley Ismael says that while the latter's father, Muley Cherif was a prisoner of Omar, Prince of Sillec, that Muley Cheriff asked Omar for a feminine companion, and Omar, "more by insult than pity, sent him one of the ugliest and most hideous black slaves he could find. From that union was born Muley Ismael."

The favorite wife of this mighty African emperor was a full-blooded Negro woman. Busnot says, "Among the most distinguished of the Sultan's wives, the first is Laila Acha, named the Empress Zidan, because she is the mother of Zidan, heir to the throne....She is black and of enormous size." (Regne de Muley Ismael, Chap. II, Rouen, 1714.)

Pidon de St. Olon, French Ambassador to Muley Ismael, says, "Upon that he (Muley Ismael) made a sign to the French slaves to approach and all threw themselves flat on their bellies at his feet."

Edith Wharton gives a graphic account of the hardships of the white slaves whom Muley Ismael used to build his city of Meknes. (In Morocco, pp. 59-74, New York, 1920.)

59. The Duchess D'Abrantes, wife of Marshal Junot, who was Napoleon's ambassador to Portugal, says of John VI, who was then Prince of Brazil, and the Regent of Portugal: "His enormous head with its Negro hair, which moreover was quite in harmony with his thick lips, his African nose, and the color of his skin." (Memoires Secretes, p. 200, Paris, 1837.) The portraits of John VI, especially a reproduction in the Bibliotheque Nationale of Paris, bear out the description of the duchess to the letter.

60. Since Pedro's father, John VI, was a Negro, it is evident that Pedro, too, was colored Moreover, Pedro's mother who was a daughter of Ferdinand VII of Spain, seems also to have been colored. The Duchess d'Abrantes says that "her skin was brown and her hair dry and woolly." (p. 207.)

Pedro I married the Archduchess Caroline Josephine, daughter of the Emperor Francis I of Austria-Hungary. His son, Pedro II, second Emperor of Brazil, was undoubtedly the most noble, most distinguished and most learned sovereign of the nineteenth century. He was first cousin to Napoleon's only son. When Pedro II visited the United States in 1876, Southern aristocracy was eager to sun itself in his presence.

Maria de Gloria, the daughter of Pedro I, married the brother of Queen Victoria's husband from which union has descended the present House of Saxe-Coburg Gotha in Germany. Recently a much heralded wedding took place between this family and the royal family of Sweden. It happened that there was a Negro strain, not too far distant, in both the bride and bridegroom, since the latter was a descendant of Bernadotte, who was colored.

For the marriages of the descendants of the Negro, John VI, and Pedro I, with other royal houses of Europe, including that of Italy, see: F. Wrangel: Les Maisons Souveraines de l'Europe, Chapters "Bragance et Portugal" and "Saxe-Coburg-Gotha." Stockholm, 1878-9.

61. Bernadotte originated in a part of France where the population has much Moorish or Negro mixture, due both to the Moorish invasion and to the settlement of Moors there after their expulsion from Spain in the 16th Century. Sir D. P. Barton says of the people in this part of France, "Their peculiar traits were traceable to their mixed ancestry which comprised French, Spanish, and Moor." (The Amazing Career of Bernadotte, p. 4, London, 1929.)

In "Bernadotte and Napoleon," Barton says, "Jean Baptiste Bernadotte, son of a lawyer at Pau, France, with a dash of Moorish blood in his Gascon veins." (p. 1, London, 1929.) By Moorish is here meant "Negro" for if Moorish were white it would have been indistinguishable from other white strain. Moreover, Bernadotte was swarthy and his hair was woolly. Henri de Rochefort, famous French journalist, attempted to prove that Bernadotte was a Jew. He said, "Bernadotte had woolly hair and a hooked nose so common among Jews." (Intermediare des Chercheurs et des Curieux, Vol. 28, p. 555, Paris, 1893.) But Bernadotte's baptismal papers proved that he was a Christian. Many Negro Moroccans of almost pure type have straight noses and even in America I have seen Aframericans with hooked noses. It is a mistake to imagine that all Negroes, even of pure stock, have flat noses. Some have faces that are Grecian in profile (Livingstone: Last Journals, Vol. I, p. 140, London, 1874.) The Peuhls, or Negro Jews of West Africa, have so-called Semitic profiles. In France, Spain and Portugal there are Negroid Jews with woolly hair. The Portuguese Jews, who are the aristocrats of Jewry, show considerable Negroid strain.

A former European diplomat in an article in the New York Sunday Tribune, entitled, "When Is a Colored Man Not A Negro in America," names several noted Europeans of Negro strain, Bernadotte amongst them. He says, "The Moorish ancestry of his (Bernadotte's) mother is a matter of local knowledge." (April 17, 1910.)

I have heard on good authority that Napoleon spoke of Bernadotte as a Mulatto, but I have not found it so far.

One day while speaking of Bernadotte, an acquaintance of mine from Southern France told me that she went to school there with one of the Bernadotte's daughters, who was so dark that she was called "La Negresse." Murat, King of Naples, and Napoleon's brother-in-law, perhaps the most spectacular figure of the Napoleonic Wars, came from this region. The Duchess d'Abrantes, who seems to have known him a little more than a faithful wife should, said of him, "There is very much of the Negro in his face," and that he looked like "a mulatto." Memoires, Vol 2, p. 238. Paris, 1835. 2 V.

Pierre Laval, former Premier of France came from near there, too. He is so evidently colored that the American newspapers mentioned it on his visit to New York. John Gunther says, "There is a strong Negroid caste of feature to many Auvergnese. Laval has thick lips, heavy, black, oily hair."—Inside Europe, p. 136.

Finally, it must not be forgotten that hundreds of thousands of Guinea Negroes were imported into Europe from 1440 to 1773 and that today not one of these pure blacks remains. Negro slavery lasted in England for 330 years (1442-1772). Where are all those hundreds of thousands of pure blacks now? Swallowed up by the white, some of whose descendants in the Southern States, boast of their pure Anglo-Saxon stock. It is a very great error to think of the Europeans as a pure white people.

62. See: A. W. Durnford: "A Soldier's Life and Work in South Africa," London, 1882.

The Illustrated London News, 1879.

C. L. Norris-Newman: In Zululand with the British throughout the War of 1879.

The New York Public Library has a file of newspaper clippings relating to the Zulu War of 1879, with abundant references to Cetewayo.

SLAVERY

63. The Century Dictionary says, "Originally one of the Slavs or Slavonians taken in war." Slav originally meant "the people of glory."

64. For the transportation of white slaves to America and their sale see, James Oneal: The Workers in American History, Chap., "The White Slave Trade." He quotes: "One ship sailing....in 1745 with 400 Germans of whom only 50 lived to see free America. Still another bearing 1500 lost 1100 from deaths on the voyage." (p. 64, New York, 1921.) Pastor Kunze, writing at that time said, "packed like herring and sold as slaves." J. B. McMaster, noted historian says of the white slaves, "The newcomer became in the eyes of the law a slave and in both the civil and the criminal code was classed with the Negro slaves and Indians....They were worked hard, were dressed in the cast off clothes of their owners and might be flogged as often as the master or mistress thought necessary." In other words, the exploiters were no respecters of color or race. (See also No. 67 of this work.)

65. For Nat Turner's insurrection see: Authentic and Impartial Narrative of the Tragical Events....Southampton County, pub. by Warner & West, 1831. Anglo-African Magazine, Vol. I, pp. 386-397 (1859).

The word "Seminole," means "runaway" or "fugitive." The Seminoles were chiefly fugitive Indian, and Negro, slaves, and corresponded to the Maroons of Jamaica, Cuba, Haiti, and South America. They fought three wars with the United States.

66. Act. V, Laws of Virginia, Oct. 1670 reads: "No Negro or Indian though baptised and enjoying their own freedom shall be capable of any such purchase of (white) Christians, but yet not debarred from buying any of their own kind." (Henings, Vol. II, p. 281.)

Act IX, Oct. 1748: "No Negro, mulatto, Indian, although a Christian or any Jew, Moor, Mohammedan....shall purchase any Christian white servants." (Hening's, Vol. V, p. 550.)

Statutes of Louisiana, Chap. 91, 13, Sec. 12, March 20, 1818, forbids the same. "It was not in fact until the year 1818 that the Legislature (of

Louisiana) found itself called upon to notice the frequency with which free persons of color bought the white stranger and in their tardy wisdom forbade any such further purchases on their part....they, however, permitted white persons of good fame and character to continue the traffic." (Quoted from Slavery Pamphlets, Vol. 23, No. 15, New York Public Library.)

67. For the sale of white people as Negro slaves, see: article from Cincinnati Philanthropist, reprinted in Colored American, June 20, 1840, where a white woman was sold as a Negro and where her ten children by two of her white masters were also sold as Negroes. For the seduction and sale of other whites as Negroes see Anglo-African Magazine, Vol. I, p. 336, (1859). Richard Hildreth, American historian says: "Just catch a stray Irish or German girl and sell her—a thing sometimes done." (A White Slave, p. 252, 5th ed.) MacCormac says: "All persons who were captured in Europe by kidnappers and sent to America were sold by the captain to the highest bidder without indenture." (Johns Hopkins Univ. Studies in Hist. and Pol. Science, Nos. 3 and 4.) This meant they could be held slaves for life like the Negroes. For the story of Sally Muller, German woman, held as a Negro, see Slavery Pamphlet, Vol. 23, No. 15, New York Public Library.

Chambers quotes, "Race! Do not speak of race; we do not mind origin and color. What we assert is that slavery whether of the blacks or whites is the regular and best condition of society. The blood of orators, generals, statesmen, even of the President of the Republic runs in the veins of men who are bought and sold like horses and mules. It is well known that many poor Anglo-American (white) children are sold as slaves. Sometimes the poor whites of the South sell their children to dealers and it is notorious that the habit of hunting for white children in the States of the North is ever increasing." Gen. Sherman wrote: "I saw men and women white as the purest Anglo-Saxon type sold like cattle." Ellison reported, "It is extraordinary to see slaves so white that you could not distinguish them from whites of the purest blood." George Fitz-Hugh of Virginia fought for the opinion that not only Negroes but all proletarian whites emigrated from Germany and Ireland should be sold as slaves for reasons of humanity." Cromwell ordered several thousand of Irish to be sold as slaves to the West Indies. Later prisoners, even political rebels were sold in large numbers as slaves. "One man in ten I knocked on the head; the rest I sold to Barbadoes," so says Cromwell. Concerning the great extent of white slavery in America, consult also, Hopp: Bundesstaat und Bundeskrieg, p. 51 (1886)—(Quoted from F. Hertz, Race and Civilization, p. 328. London, 1928, trans. Levetus & Entz.)

C. M. McInnes says of the West Indies, "The white servants were often placed under black overseers who treated them with particular barbarity. As the blacks born in the islands acquired a knowledge of handicrafts, the white servants were compelled to do the roughest, hardest work in the fields." An Introduction to the Economic History of the British Empire, pp. 31-5. London, 1935.

For much additional data, see: Chapter, "White People Sold as Negro Slaves," in Sex and Race, Vol. II. 1942.

68. For Prince Abd-El-Rahman, see Michaud: "Biographie Universelle" of famous men, Vol. I, p. 45.

69. The U. S. Census of 1790 showed 195 Negro slaveholders, of whom 6 were in Connecticut, and 9 in New York. In 1830 there were about 4,500 Negro slave-holders. In 1836, slaves owned by Negroes in New Orleans numbered 640. On Negro slave-holders, see: Popular Science Monthly, Oct.

1912. C. G. Woodson: "Free Negro Owners of Slaves," gives the names of the slave-holders.

70. The British Emancipation Proclamation allowed the masters to keep their slaves as apprentices. They were not really free until 1838.

Lincoln's Emancipation Proclamation permitted the retention of the slaves in those slave states which were fighting for the Union as well as in those parishes and counties in sympathy with him. He also excluded Tennessee, hoping that it would join the Union. In the words of the Proclamation these states were to continue holding their slaves "precisely as if this proclamation were not issued." (Proclamation of January 1, 1863.)

Slavery was abolished, not by the Emancipation Proclamation, but by the Thirteenth Amendment on Dec. 31, 1865, eight months after Lincoln's death.

71. That both Negroes and whites are still held as slaves in North Africa is well-known to those who have lived in those lands. As for Arabia of which I know little, I have had this information from reliable personal sources, one of my informants being the son of an Irish diplomat who lived until recently in Arabia with his father. Also W. B. Seabrook relates, "I have seen on the desert edge a black Moslem slave riding bejewelled in gold-embroidered robes among white Christian girls and women who toiled for him barefooted in the fields." My friends replied, "Stuff and nonsense, Mansour, though a slave, was one of the richest members of the tribe." Adventures in Arabia, p. 90, New York, 1928.

Rosita Forbes, in the chapter, "The Slave Market—Arabia," tells of the white women slaves one of whom "might have been born anywhere north.... even of the English Channel" and of "Circassians....of a fairness ranging from ivory to olive."—Women Called Wild, p. 28-48, N. Y., 1937.

Ameer Rihani said in 1928, "You have seen with your eyes—even slaves and slave-girls. He, (the sultan), has Christian girls also. Ask him for one. He will present one to you." (The Maker of Modern Arabia, pp. 152-153.) By Christian is meant "white." The blacks are either Mohammedan or pagan. The former comes from Armenia, and Georgia in the Caucasus; the black ones from Abyssinia and the Sudan. See also article by Capt. L. H. Blood on North Africa in N. Y. Evening Journal, Aug. 10, 1934.

SPORTS

72. See the Autobiography of "Major" Taylor, Worcester, Mass., 1928, with reproductions of newspaper articles, etc.

73. For a partial list of these athletes, see: Negro Year Book, 1937-38, pp. 14-18. Tuskegee Institute.

WARFARE — COMMANDERS

74. "The two greatest colored figures in the history of Islam are (1) Bilal of Ethiopia....(2)Tarik-bin-Ziad. He also was a slave and became a great general in Islam and was the commander of the Moorish Army which invaded Spain. Jebel-u-Tarik (the mountain of Tarik), that is, Gibraltar, is named after him. One of the greatest Turkish classics is called 'Tarik-bin-Ziad," and has him as its hero." (Mme. Halideh-Edib, leading Turkish writer on Turkish Negroes from her letter in my possession.)

Morgan says, "This brave and fortunate Moor said to be Moussas's own slave has rendered his name immortal to all posterity." (History of Barbary and Algiers, p. 160 (1728.)

75. "Hannibal, who died with the rank of commander-in-chief, was a Negro bought in Constantinople." (D. M. Wallace: Russia, p. 271.) Also Albert Parry: Abraham Hannibal, Journal of Negro History, Oct. 1923.

76. Napoleon said at St. Helena, "It would have been much more proper for Toussaint to have been returned to France as a general of division than as a criminal." (Historical Miscellanies, Vol. I, p. 215. London, 1823.)

77. Gragnon-LaCoste in his "Life of Toussaint L'Overture," names the sum as 6,000,000 francs, and says: "Girard, to give him his true name, never returned the millions entrusted to his care following the events which deprived Toussaint of his liberty." This writer tells also of the litigation that followed in the courts for the money left by Girard to the city of Philadelphia. (p. 203, Paris, 1877.)

For Girard's jim-crow will see J. B. McMaster's, Stephen Girard, Vol. II, p. 450, Philadelphia, 1918.

78. Gen. Pamphile La Croix, (white), who fought against the Emperor Dessalines in Haiti, said, "Jean Francois, raised still higher recently to the rank of grandee....sailed with his officers to Spain to enjoy the favors of the Court of Madrid, where was reserved for him all the high honors of his rank, the titles and decorations, and emoluments of a captain-general." (La Revolution de St. Domingue, Vol. I, pp. 300, 304.)

79. For mention of these generals, see: Ardouin: Etudes sur L'Histoire d'Haiti, Vol. V, p. 10; D. A. Molza; Les Negres, p. 175; Napoleon's Correspondence, Vol. IV, p. 252; V. Schoelcher: Toussaint L'Ouverture, pp. 439-442; and W. H. Ferris: The African Abroad, p. 934, New Haven, 1913.

80. Consult: R. T. Wingate: Ten Years' Captivity in the Mahdi's Camp, London, 1892.

Slatin Pasha: Fire and Sword in the Sudan, London, 1896.

R. A. Bermann: The Mahdi of Allah, London, 1931.

81. In the Philippines, "the Negroes deserted in scores and for the purpose of joining the insurgents and many of them, like the celebrated Fagan, became leaders and fought the white troops or their former comrades with zest and ability." (The Negro Soldier in War and Peace: North American Review, Vol. 185, p. 326, June, 1907.)

82. General A. A. Dodds, conqueror of Dahomey, and France's greatest colonial soldier, was born in St. Louis, Senegal, West Africa, of mulatto parentage on both sides of his family. In color he was very dark. The New York Tribune, April 17, 1910, said that he was so popular that he could easily have seized the power in France as "the entire nation irrespective of party or politics turned out to welcome him and to such an extent did he become an object of popular enthusiasm that there is no doubt that he might easily have established himself in the role of military dictator had it not been for his loyalty to the republic," yet it adds, he "would not have been permitted to drink at the same bar with a white man (in America) and in many states of the Union would not be permitted to ride in the same street car." Gen. Dodds was a Grand Officer of the Legion of Honor, the highest possible grade in that order. He died in 1922.

See F. Desplantes: Le General Dodds; Larousse Mensuel, Oct. 1922; and all works on the conquest of Dahomey.

83. For a double page picture of Naval Captain Mortenol as commander of the Air Defenses of Paris with his officers, together with a summary of his work, see "L'Illustration" of Paris, March 22, 1919, pp. 319-27. I knew Commander Mortenol personally and visited and talked with him a good deal at his home at 5 rue Francois-Coppee, Paris. Mortenol was a Commander of the Legion of Honor, the same rank held by Marshals Foch and Haig and General Pershing in that order at that time.

84. That Col. Batista, commander-in-chief of the Cuban army, is a mulatto has several times been stated in the American newspapers. Karl Decker says, "Sergt. Fulgencio Batista, a chino-mulatto." (N. Y. American, Oct. 22, 1933.) The word, mulatto, when used with "chino" is superfluous. A chino is the offispring of a mulatto and an Indian.

WARFARE — MEN

85. For the exploits of the Negro in the earlier American Wars, see L. E. Wilkes: Missing Pages in American History, Washington, D. C., 1919. Consult also: E. M. Scott: American Negro in the World War, p. 259. Chicago, 1919.

(The men on page 49 are three of the 41 Negro winners of the Congressional Medal of Honor awarded by Congress for the highest bravery in action; and one of the three winners of the Victoria Cross, Britain's most coveted decoration for valor. The first three from top to bottom are Sergt.-Major C. A. Fleetwood, Grand Army veteran; John S. Lawson, U. S. N.; and Sergt. George H. Wanton of the Spanish-American War, of Washington, D. C. The fourth is William Hall, native of Nova Scotia, of the British navy. No Negroes were awarded either medal in the first or second world wars.)

86. On March 26, 1863, Lincoln wrote Johnson, "The colored population is the great available and yet unavailed of force for saving the Union."

To J. C. Conkling, August 26, 1863, he said, "The emancipation policy and the use of the colored troops constitute the heaviest blow yet dealt to rebellion and that at least one of these important successes could not have been achieved when it was but for the aid of the colored troops."

To John T. Mills, August 1864, "The slightest knowledge of arithmetic will prove to any man that the rebel armies cannot be destroyed by Democratic strategy. It would sacrifice all the white men of the North to do it. There are now in the service of the United States nearly 150,000 colored men, most of them under arms, defending and acquiring Union territory. The Democratic strategy demands that these forces be disbanded and that the masters be conciliated by restoring them to slavery....Abandon all posts now garrisoned by black men, take the 150,000 men from our side and put them in the battlefield or cornfield against us and we would be compelled to abandon the war in three weeks."

To Chas. D. Robinson, August 17, 1864, "Drive back to the support of the rebellion the physical force which the colored people now give and promise us and neither the present nor any coming administration can save the Union....The party who elect a President on a War and Slavery Restoration would, of necessity, lose the colored force; and that force being lost, would be as powerless to save the Union as to do any other impossible thing."

"It is not a question of sentiment or taste but one of physical force which may be measured and estimated as horse-power and steampower are measured and estimated." To J. M. Schermerhorn, Sept. 12, 1864, he adds emphatically as regards this Negro balance of power, "Keep it, and you can save the Union. Throw it away, and the Union goes with it." Speeches, Letters, and State Papers, Nicolay & Hay, 1922.

87. These are the official figures. See W. F. Fox: Regimental Losses in the American Civil War, p. 532, Albany, N. Y. 36,847 colored soldiers lost their lives in the Civil War, which was phenomenally high. For "Colored Troops," see Chapter VI.

88. See Negro Year Book, p. 329 (1931-32), Tuskegee Institute. N. Y. Globe, June 2, 1910.

89. B. Mitre: Paginas de la Historia, Chap. IV,—Falucho—pp. 12-15, Buenos Aires, 1906.

V. Blasco Ibanez: Argentina y sus Grandezas, has a reproduction of Falucho's monument. (p. 285, Madrid, 1910.)

90. "First American soldiers of any race, white or black, to receive the French Croix de Guerre were Henry Johnson of Albany, N. Y., and Needham Roberts of Trenton, N. J." (E. J. Scott: The American Negro in the World War, p. 256.)

MISCELLANEOUS

91. For the history of the word, "Niger" and "Nigritia" from which "Negro" comes, see Sir William Smith's Dictionary of Greek and Roman Geography, Vol. II, p, 429, as well as pp. 296-7. Also Journal Royal Soc., Vol. II, pp. 1-28 (1832) by W. M. Leake, who says with regard to the African origin of "Niger," "More than one celebrated writer have fallen into the error of supposing 'Niger,' a Latin word." Also Sir Rufus Donkine, "The Niger," pp. 16, 144; and Gerald Massey, "A Book of the Beginnings," Vol. III, p. 610. For the origin of "Ethiopia," see Vol. I, p. 36 of the latter work.

"Black" and "colored" on the other hand, have no historic meaning whatever for African peoples. Black, from the Anglo-Saxon, blaec, has most horrible meanings. See any large dictionary. "Colored" is related to the Latin, celare, to conceal, to color up, to paint a thing other than in its true light. Thus the tendency to decry "Negro" on the ground that it means "slavery" is sheer ignorance. For instance, a Negro newspaper took a poll of its readers some years ago and they chose "colored." But the jim-crow car, that greatest degrader of American citizenship is usually marked "colored." The majority of this paper's circulation is in the South. Did they choose "colored" so as to be in line with the jim-crow policy? Still another paper used "race-man," which makes the uninitiated think of the race-track. Another very racial group, chooses "black" which, as was said, is positively a white man's word.

Of course, there is only one race—the human race. But of all the names used by the stronger group in America to set the dark-skinned citizen apart, Negro is the least objectionable. Not only is it very ancient but it has a record in America of four centuries of fortitude, endurance, and survival power, rare in the annals of mankind. "Negro" is making splendid progress towards prestige in such terms as Negro spirituals, Negro boxer, Negro music, Negro athlete, Negro soldier, Negro loyalty.

There is not a single noted name that was not once used in contempt or is still even so used in parts of the world. Christian, Anglo-Saxon, Scotch, Irish, English, American, Yankee, all were once very much looked down on.

Shakespeare's use of Negro deals with miscegenation. Merchant of Venice, III, v. 42.

I have dealt more at length on this subject in an article called, "What Shall We Call Ourselves?"

92. For the word "admiral," consult the Century Dictionary. The exploits of these black sea-rovers date back to the Phoenicians, who roamed as far as the British Isles. The captain of the pirates that captured Julius Caesar was a Negro, and so was one of his lieutenants. J. Gollomb says of them, "Spartaco (the leader)....was a mongrel of black, brown and white races....One of his lieutenants, was a Negro of many breeds, Micio." (Pirates, Old and New, p. 11. London, 1931.)

In the 14th Century the fleets of Abu Hassan Ali, "The Black Sultan," greatest of the Merindes monarchs of Morocco, dominated the Mediterranean. On August 4, 1340, he won a complete victory over the Christians led by the Admiral of Castille, Godfrey Tenorio. (Biographie Universelle, Vol. I, p. 80.) Abu Hassan Ali's mother was an Abyssinian slave, and his father, a dark mulatto.

G. Hardy says, "Masters of North Africa, the Merindes profited by their maritime situation to create a powerful fleet and to undertake against the Christian countries of the Mediterranean, a savage struggle.

"From their ports, left armed ships manned by men of proved bravery and maintained by kinds of communal societies. These 'corsairs' descended unexpectedly upon the coasts or the isles of the Mediterranean, and they captured and sold as slaves the sailors and the passengers. A veritable terror reigned in the Mediterranean....They ravaged the coasts of Portugal, Spain, Southern France—and even went as far as Britain." (Les Grands Etapes de l'Histoire du Maroc, pp. 50-54, Paris, 1921.)

In Chap. XI of Candide, Voltaire tells of a Negro sea-rover, who captured the daughter of Pope Urban X and the Princess of Palestrina of Italy. This black captain condescended to make the beautiful princess his mistress. In relating her story, the princess speaks of him as "an abominable Negro who believed he was conferring a great honor on me."

Writing in 1801, Lempriere says, of the Salee rovers, "They were for a long time the terror of the commerce of Europe. As dreaded for their audacity as their cruelty, they made themselves the masters of the Ocean." (Voyages dans L'Empire du Maroc, p. 46.)

The United States of America was forced to pay tribute to these African sea-rovers until its victory over them in 1815. S. Lane-Poole, Story of the Barbary Corsairs, p. 258. N. Y., 1890. These sea-rovers were largely Negro. Lane-Poole says they were called "niggers," p. 304. Holland, Sweden, Denmark, and Spain also had to pay them tribute to sail, especially on the Mediterranean.

93. The staff correspondent of La Depeche Coloniale of Paris, sent the following from Berlin on August 25, 1931: "The Negro, whom William of Prussia Adopted as a Son, has Just Died In an Insane Asylum." The article relates how the Negro boy, later christened Henri Noel, was presented to William I. by Rohlfs, African explorer, in 1867, how the emperor gave him a military education; how, while engaged as an officer, at the battle of Plevna, he received a wound in the head that made him insane and how he was interned in an asylum at Ancona, Italy, where he was completely inoffensive, though he suffered from delusions of grandeur. "Until 1918," the article continues, "the royal court of Prussia, paid for the maintenance of Henri Noel, through the Italian Embassy. Kaiser Wilhelm II interested himself particularly in the welfare of Henri. After the war, the German Government paid for his care.

"In the paintings of 1867 to 1870 one may see a superb young Negro in the suite of William of Prussia: that is the poor lunatic of Ancona."

94. Paul Cuffe sailed his own ship, "The Traveler," with a Negro crew and Negro emigrants, between the United States and West Africa, see, S. R. B. Ahuma: Memoirs of West African Celebrities, Liverpool, 1905, and John W. Cromwell, Negro in American History, Washington, 1914.

On Major Martin R. Delany, see, F. A. Rollin: Life and Public Service of Martin R. Delany.

Benjamin (Pap) Singleton, "The Moses of the Colored Exodus," was really an amazing figure. He succeeded in settling 10,000 or more Negroes from the South, in Kansas. Later, when the whites there opposed him he founded "The United Transatlantic Society" for taking them to Africa. (Amer. Jour. of Sociol., July, 1909, p. 78.)

For William Ellis, see A. M. E. Church Review, Vol. 20, p. 302; Vol. 22, pp. 250-54.

Chief Sam, "The Gold Coast Messiah," bought the ship, "Curityba," for $60,000 to take the Negroes "back" to Africa. N. Y. Times, Feb. 26, 1914. His ship went down off the coast of Africa but the crew and passengers were saved.

For Dr. Thorne, N. Y. World, July 29, 1922.

For Marcus Garvey, consult N. Y. Times Index from 1921 onwards; Reader's Guide to Periodical Literature from the same period; and Garvey's own paper, "The Negro World."

95. See: The New York Evening Journal, July 3, 1907. (Reproduced in the Baltimore Afro-American, July 8, 1933.)

96. Booker T. Washington said, "One lecture bureau offered me $50,000 ....I replied that my life-work was at Tuskegee." (Up from Slavery, p. 226, New York, 1901.)

97. See "A Voice From Harper's Ferry," by O. P. Anderson, one of the Negroes who aided John Brown, p. 35, Boston, 1861. Also B. J. Stutler: Capt. John Brown, Harper's Ferry, 1930.

98. The Nubians, or unmixed Negroes of Ancient Egypt, used hot irons, not to straighten their hair, but to arrange it in rows of small curls all around the head. P. Perdrizet says, "Whilst the Egyptians shaved the head carefully, the Ethiopians permitted their thick woolly hair to grow and with a great effort of hot irons and cosmetics arranged it in tiers of curls." (Bronzes Grecs de l'Egypte, p. 58, Paris, 1911.)

99. The various U. S. census reports consistently show that Aframericans are longer lived than white Americans. In 1900 there were 837 whites who had reached the age of one hundred and over, and there were 2553 Negroes, or 30 to 1 in favor of the Negroes. In 1910 the whites were 764 and the Negroes, 2675, or 35 to 1. In 1920, whites: 1168; Negroes, 2935 or 25 to 1. In 1930, whites: 1180; Negroes, 2467, or 19 to 1 The Negro's span of life, like that of the white's is evidently being burnt up by his progress. (U. S. Census Reports, 1920, Vol. II, p. 158, and 1930, Vol. II, p. 577). It is very likely, too, that some of the Negroes exaggerated their longevity Many old persons do. However, the U. S. Cenus, even when wrong, is the nearest we have to accuracy on the subject. The 1830 census showed 2,120 Negro centenarians to 531 white. Centenarians among Negro women outnumber the Negro men two to one.

100. Speaking of the parade of the Negro Brotherhood in Sevilie, Spain, in 1926, Arthur Schomburg, curator of the Carnegie Library, West 135th Street, New York City, says, "It was only human to wish to examine the garments of the Brotherhood of the Negroes after observing the similarity to the white robes and cowls used by the Ku Klux Klan of our country. To all appearances the American organization copied the dress of those believers in Christ. Not even in garments, it seems, is the American order original. They are evidently copied faithfully from a very sacred brotherhood whose devotion won them the love and gratitude of the Spanish people from King to peasant, Pontiff to believer." (Opportunity Maga, p. 164, June, 1927, New York.)

Today the descendants of these Spanish Negroes are quite bleached from mixing with their white neighbors. But the old Negro traditions remain. The Negro church of Nuestra Senora de Los Angeles in the Barrio Carmona is still maintained by them. Priests, guides, and others in Seville informed me that the garb is exactly like that of centuries ago. For earlier information on these Negritos, as they are called in Seville, see Zuniga's Annales de Sevilla, published in Madrid in 1677. Later the Negroes rose to a position of prominence and had a Count, after whom one of the streets is still named.

If the originators of the Ku Klux Klan did not copy the garb of these Negroes then the coincidence is really amazing.

Picture below is parade of Seville Negro order.

For additional data on nearly all these Facts, see the three volumes of Sex and Race.

THE END.

LIST OF WORLD'S GREATEST MEN AND WOMEN OF AFRICAN DESCENT

by J. A. Rogers

KINGS QUEENS, PRESIDENTS

HATSHEPSUT, Ablest Queen of Far Antiquity, Egypt.

MAKEDA, Queen of Sheba, Consort of King Solomon. Ethiopia.

CLITUS, King of Bactria, Foster-Brother of Alexander the Great.

MASSINISSA, King of Numidia, Rival of Hannibal.

CLEOPATRA, Queen of Egypt.

ZENOBIA, Beautiful Queen of Palmyra. Asia Minor.

ABRAHA, Ethiopia's First Christian Ruler.

KAFUR THE MAGNIFICENT, King of Egypt.

NICEPHORUS PHOCAS, Greatest of the Byzantine Rulers. Greece.

ABU HASSAN ALI, the Black Sultan of Morocco.

ASKIA THE GREAT, Emporor of Timbuctoo.

ALESSANDRO DIE MEDICI, Duke of Florence.

ANNE ZINGHA, Fiery Queen of Matamba, West Africa.

MALIK AMBAR, Sultan of the Deccan, India.

MALIK ANDEEL, Benevolent Sultan of Bengal, India.

MULAI ISMAEL, Most Extraordinary Ruler of the 18th Century. Morrocco.

OSETI TUTU, Founder of the Ashanti Nation, West Africa.

JOHN VI, King of Portugal and Maker of Modern Brazil.

PEDRO I, First Emperor of Brazil.

PEDRO II, Brazil's Learned Emperor.

MOSHESH, Warrier, Statesman, King. South Africa.

GENERAL BOYER, President of Haiti's Golden Age.

CETEWAYO, Zulu King and Victor over the British.

KHAMA THE GOOD, King of Basutoland, South Africa.

BEHANZIN, African Poet-King, Who Defied France. Dahomey, West Africa.

MENELIK II, "Ever-Victorious Lion of Judah," Ethiopia.

PREMPEH OF THE GOLDEN STOOL, King of Ashanti, West Africa.

H. E. NILO-PECANHA, President of Brazil.

CARLOS A. MENDOZA, President of Panama.

HAILE SELASSIE, Emperor of Ethiopia.

DICTATORS

BASHIR AGHASSI, Eunuch, Ruler of the Turkish Empire for 24 years.

DESSALINES THE FEROCIOUS, First Emperor of Haiti.

CHRISTOPHE, Henry I of Haiti.

SOULOUQUE THE BUTCHER, President of Haiti.

CARLOS LOPEZ, Tyrant of Paraguay.

FRANCISCO LOPEZ II, Tyrant of Paraguay

ULISES HEUREAUX, Iron-Handed Ruler of Santo Domingo.

BU AHMED, Iron Chancellor of Morocco. 1900.

LUIS SANCHEZ CERRO, Despot of Peru, 1930–33.

CONQUERORS

THOTMES III, the Napoleon of Far Antiquity.

PIANKHI OF ETHIOPIA, Conqueror of Egypt.

ABRAHA AL-ASHRAM, Emproer of Yemen, Arabia.

YUSUF I, Sultan of Africa, Conqueror of Spain. 1806 A.D.

SONNI ALI, Founder of the Empire of Timbuctoo.

CHAKA, Zulu King, "The Great Elephant."

SAMORY, "Napoleon of the Sudan."

RAGAH ZOBEIR, Africa's Champion Against White Invasion.

GREAT PATRIOTS

CAPTAIN CUDJOE, The William Tell of Jamaica, West Indies.

INVENTORS

JAN ERNEST MATZELIGER, who revolutionized the Shoe Industry;
GRANVILLE WOODS, Originator of the Third Rail.

AFRAMERICAN RACIAL LEADERS

FREDERICK DOUGLASS, Champion of Human Rights.
MONROE TROTTER, the St. Francis of Aframerican Leaders.
MARCUS GARVEY, Back-to-Africa Leader.
A. PHILIP RANDOLPH, Labor Leader.
FINLEY WILSON, Little Napoleon of Elkdom.
MARY McLEOD BETHUNE, Educator and Leader.

PAINTERS AND SCULPTORS

THEODORE CHASSERIAU of Haiti, French Portrait Painter.
EDWARD M. BANNISTER, American Painter.
HENRY O. TANNER, Foremost Modern Painter of Religious Subjects.
AUGUSTA SAVAGE, Aframerican Sculptress.
RICHMOND BARTHE, Sculptor.

SINGERS, MUSICIANS, COMPOSERS

IBRAHIM AL-MAHDI, Caliph of Islan, Brohter of Haroun-Al-Raschid.
CHEVALIER DE ST. GEORGES, Violinist, Composer, Swordsman.
JOSE D. BRINDIS DE SALA, German Court Violinist and Baron.
CARLOS GOMES, Brazilian Opera Composer.
SAMUEL COLEREDGE-TAYLOR, Musical Genius of England.
ROLAND HAYES, Exquisite Singer of Love Songs.
PAUL ROBESON, Athletic and Musical Prodigy.
WILLIAM C. HANDY, Father of the Blues.
WILLIAM GRANT STILL, Operatic Composer.
NATHANIEL DETT, Composer.
MARIAN ANDERSON, "The Voice of A Century."

SWORDSMEN

JEAN LOUIS of France, perhaps the World's Greatest Duelist; and others.

PRIZE-FIGHTERS

PETER JACKSON, The Chivalrous.
JACK JOHNSON, Supreme Athlete of his Time.
JOE GANS, " The Old Master."
JOE LOUIS, "The Black Bomber."

ACTORS

IRA ALDRIDGE, Greatest of the Othellos.
MORGAN SMITH of Philadelphia, Shakespearean Idol.
CHOCOLAT, Great French Comedian.
BERT WILLIAMS, King of Laughter.
JOSEPHINE BAKER, The Toast of Paris, France.

POLITICAL LEADERS

EUGENE CHEN, Dynamic Foreign Minister of China.
BLAISE DIAGNE, Orator and French Cabinet Minister.
GRATIEN CANDACE, Vice-President, Chamber of Deptuies.
NAHAS PASHA, Leader of the Wafd, or Home Rule Party of Egypt, and Prime Minister of Egypt.

LEGAL LIGHTS

SIR CONRAD REEVES, Cheif Justice of Barbadoes.
SIR SAMUEL LEWIS, Chief Justice of Sierra Leone.

EXPLORERS

ESTEVANICO, discoverer of Arizona and New Mexico.
PAUL DU CHAILLU, Discoverer of The Gorilla.
MATTHEW HENSON, First Person to Reach the North Pole.

NAT TURNER, Leader of America's Greatest Slave Revolt.
TOUSSAINT L'OUVERTURE of Haiti.
LOUIS DELGRES of Guadeloupe, Who Defied Napoleon.
VINCENTE GUERRERO, Liberator of Mexico and President
BAMBAATA, Leader of Revolt Against British Rule. So. Africa.

GREAT GENERALS

HANNIBAL OF CARTHAGE, Father of Military Strategy.
ZAID BIN HARITH, Adopted Son of Mohamet
ST. MARUICE, Saing of the Catholic Church.
ABRAHAM HANNIBAL, Commander-in-Chief of the Russian Army.
ENRIQUE DIAS, Liberator of Brazil from Holland.
ALEXANDER DUMAS, Napoleon's Dashing Cavalry Leader.
BERTRAND DU GUESCLIN, Liberator of France from the English.
ALEXANDER PETION, President of Haiti.
CARLOS MANUEL PIAR, of Venezuela, Boliver's Greatest General.
ALFRED A. DODDS, France's Leading Colonial Soldier.
S. H. MORTENOL, Naval Captain, Chief of the Air Defenses of Paris. 1917–18.

RELIGIOUS LEADERS

AKHENATON, Most Remarkable of the Pahraohs.
ST. GEORGE, Patron Saint of England.
BENEDICT THE MOOR, Catholic Saint.
ANTONIO VIERA, Portugal's Most Splendid Personage.
SAMUEL ADJAI CROWTHER, Explorer and Bishop of the Niger.

WRITERS

LOKMAN, Wisest Man of the Ancient East.
ESOP, the Great Fabulist.
TERRENCE, Prince of the Latin Stylists.
ANTAR, the Homer of Arabia.
AL-JAHIZ, Lord of the Golden Age of Arab Literature.
JUAN LATINO, "The Master," Latin Scholar.
ALEXANDER PUSHKIN, Russian Poet.
ALEXANDER DUMAS, the World's Greatest Romancer.
ALEXANDER DUMAS, Fils, Father of the Modern French Theatre.
PAUL LAURANCE DUNBAR, Apostle of Beauty.
PLACIDO, Cuba's Martyr-Poet.
MACHADO DE ASSIS, Litterateur of Brazil.
W. E. B. DUBOIS, Scholar, Educator, Agitator for Human Rights.
GEORGE S. SCHUYLER, Satirist and Original Thinker.

EDUCATORS

EDWARD W. BLYDEN, Statesman and Patriot.
BOOKER T. WASHINGTON, Leader in Industrial Education.
HUBERT HARRISON, Intellectual Phenomenon and Lecturer.
CARTER G. WOODSON, Founder of the Assn. for the Study of Negro Life and History.

PHYSICANS

IMHOTEP, God of Medicine. Egypt.
James Derham, Daniel Williams, and other Aframericans.
JOSE T. DE SOUSA MARTINS, Sanitary Expert of Portugal.

SCIENTISTS

RICHARD HILL, Naturalist of Jamaica, West Indies.
GEORGE WAHSINGTON CARVER, Agricultural Wizard of Tuskegee.
ERNEST JUST, Pioneer in Biology.

FINANCIERS

C. C. SPAULDING of Durham, N. C. and others.

OTHER OUTSTANDING FACTS OF NEGRO PROGRESS

AWARDS. Dr. Ralph Bunche was awarded the Nobel Peace Prize, world's highest honor in that field, in 1950 for his work in ending war between Israel and the Arab nations.

Gwendolyn Brooks of Chicago won the Pulitzer Prize for poetry, America's highest honor in that field, in 1949; also the $1,000 prize of the Academy of Arts and Letters.

Roy F. Eaton of New York City won the coveted Chopin Prize of $2,000 offered by the Kosciusko Foundation as the best pianist in a nation-wide competition.

William H. Moses of Hampton Institute Engineering Department won first prize for the best design for Virginia's exhibit in the New York's World Fair, 1939-40.

William Grant Still won first prize in an international competition for the theme song of the New York World Fair, 1939-40. The theme song was played several times daily to millions.

Philippa Duke Schuyler of New York City in a young people's contest in 1946 for the best musical competition in the two Americas offered by the Detroit Symphony Orchestra won first prize with her "Rumpelstiltskin" and the second prize with "Manhattan Nocturne."

ARMED FORCES. The ratio of Negroes inducted into the armed forces during World War II was 10.7, or more than one per cent higher than the white. Negroes were 1,154,720. There were 8,600 Negro officers, including one brigadier-general; 206,512 served in the Pacific; 225,367 in Europe and North Africa; and 23,892 in China, India, and Burma.

Over 6,000 Negroes served in the Air Force in World War II. Of these there were 925 officers (685 of whom were pilots); 657 radio operators; 379 crew chiefs; and 88 radar technicians.

Eighty-one aviators won the Distinguished Flying Cross, America's second highest decoration for valor, in World War II. The first was Capt. Charles B. Hall, who shot down a German P. 40 Warhawk in Italy in 1943.

Chief Petty Officer Graham W. Jackson was credited with being the individual who sold the highest number of War Bonds in World War II, or a total of $2,000,000. A skilled pianist and accordionist he was very popular at bond rallies. He was given six Treasury awards and appeared in several concerts at the White House.

Three Negroes won the Congressional Medal of Honor, America's highest decoration, in the Korean War. They are: Pfc. William Thompson, and Sergt. Cornelius Charlton, both of New York City; and William R. Charette, Navy hospital corpsman of Ludington, Mich. They are the first to receive this honor since the Spanish-American War due to color discrimination in the award. (See No. 85.)

CONGRESS. Negroes returned to the Congress of the United States in 1931 after an absence of 30 years. They are Oscar DePriest of Chicago, 1931-35; Arthur Mitchell of Chicago, 1935-43; and William L. Dawson of Chicago; Adam

Powell of New York; and Charles C. Diggs, Jr. of Detroit who are now there (1955).

EDUCATION. Negro illiteracy which was 30 per cent in 1910 is less than 7 per cent in 1955. It has not only almost disappeared in the North but in some areas it is less than white illiterary as in New York.

In 1950, Negro colleges had a total of 71,000 students; a property value of over $50,000,000, and an endowment of $59,091,395. Nearly all were in the South. 553 Negroes had a Doctor's Degree.

More than 230 Negroes now teach in leading white universities in the North. One of the most noted was Dr. William A. Hinton, recently retired professor of the Harvard Medical School and one of the world's leading authorities on syphilis.

FINANCE. The latest figures (1951) give 14 large Negro banks with assets of $35,000,000; and 24 savings and loan companies with assets of $16,404,918. Negro purchasing power in 1954 was estimated at $17,500,000,000, or an increase of 250 per cent since 1945.

The 60 leading insurance companies had $1,287,216,075.10 insurance in force; had paid out $13,742,016.88; had assets of $137,708,766; and an annual income of $60,684,609.

JUDICIAL. In 1955, Harold A. Stevens of New York, native of South Carolina, was appointed a Justice of the New York State Supreme Court. He is the second Negro in American history to hold a Supreme Court justiceship. The first is Jonathan Jasper Wright, who was elected to that office in South Carolina in 1870 and served until 1877.

In 1954, John Edward Carberry was appointed Chief Justice of Jamaica, British West Indies; and Jose Maria Vasquez Diaz, Chief Justice of the Republic of Panama. They are the first of their color to hold that highest judicial office.

SCIENCE: American Men of Science, leading authority in that field, lists more than 129 Negroes outstanding in medicine, engineering, inventions, architecture, etc.

Six Negro scientists helped in the making of the first atomic bomb. One was J. Ernest Wilkins, one of the world's leading mathematicians, who earned his Ph.D. at the age of seventeen.

SPORTS. In 1928, an Algerian Negro, El Ouafi, won the Marathon, greatest feature of the Olympic games at Amsterdam in the record time of 2 hours 32 minutes, and 22.6 seconds for the 26 miles.

Negroes have always shone in the Olympics. In track and field there have been winners as Eddie Tolan, Harrison Dillard, Jesse Owens, Mal Whitfield, Alice Coachman, Arthur Wint and John Woodruff. In 1952, John Davis won the heavyweight lifting title and in other international contests emerged as the world's strongest man. In 1954, Willie Mays with .345 led as the champion batter in baseball. In 1957 Althea Gibson won the Wimbledon championship and was given a ticker-tape parade in New York.

MISCELLANEOUS. An outstanding fact of Negro progress may be seen in comparison with the Russian slaves, who were freed in 1861, or four years earlier than the American Negro. In 1911, the 14,000,000 descendants of Russian slaves had an estimated $500,000,000 in property, or about $36 per capita. The 10,000,000 descendants of Negro slaves had after 50 years of freedom, $700,000,000 or $70 per capita. And while the Russians had 70 per cent illiteracy; the Negro had 30.

An official postage stamp of the Vatican State, of which Pope Pius is head, has the Virgin Mary as a Negro woman on it. It is a recent issue and is of several denominations. A recent postage stamp of Spain has on it the celebrated Black Virgin of Montserrat, Spain, and Child.

HENRY N. GEORGE. Won Congressional Medal of Honor for "life-saving from the perils of the deep." A ferry-boat worker, he went to the rescue of excursionists on the ill-fated General Slocum, June 15, 1904, saving 25 lives, 1,061 were lost. Awarded also Gold Medal of the City of New York. Lost an eye in World War I in engagement with German submarine. Lives in Jamaica, N. Y.

A TRUTH SUPPRESSED FOR 333 YEARS

(1619-1952)

NOW TOLD IN STARTLING NEW BOOK

By J. A. ROGERS

Author: "SEX AND RACE," "FROM SUPERMAN TO MAN," and other fearless works

Negro Ancestry in the White Race

Thanks to the slaveholders of America, belief that the Negro has contributed nothing to world civilization has come to be an accepted fact. Great white scientists and even Negro scholars are among those who accept this myth without question.

For instance, Prof. Arnold J. Toynbee, often called the world's greatest living historian, echoes this belief. In his six-volume work, "A Study of History," published 1934-1939, he says, Vol. 1, pp. 233-238:

"When we classify Mankind by color the only one of the primary races . . . which has not made a creative contribution to any of our 21 civilizations is the Black Race. . . .

"Within the first 6000 years the Black Race has not helped create any civilization. . . ."

A most astounding statement from a Master of History! And it carries great weight because Prof. Toynbee is a sincere opponent of race prejudice.

However, there are mountains of evidence to disprove him. This evidence is scattered in thousands of ancient books and may be seen in old paintings and sculpture; also in more recent books of which very little is said or heard. But now J. A. Rogers who has been collecting these facts for nearly forty years has woven them, together with pictures, into a connected story, entitled:

"NATURE KNOWS NO COLOR-LINE"

RESEARCH INTO

The Negro Ancestry in the White Race

Starting with ancient Egypt and coming down through Greece and Rome this book shows what the Negro has contributed, especially to Western European civilization, to the present. For instance, there were the Moors, who invaded Europe 711 A.D. and were the dominant power there for the next 500 years. Writings and painting of those times show them as jet-black and with wooly hair. The Moors gave Europe one of its finest civilizations and rescued it from the Dark Ages.

Not only have the Negroes contributed science and art to Europe but since they were once dominant their "blood" entered into that of the whites and some were ancestors of Europe's leading families, including royal ones from Italy to Scandinavia.

How many know that England had been absorbing Negroes not only since the Roman invasion of B.C. 55, *but over a thousand years before?*

How many know that Negro slavery lasted in England for 434 *years* (1440-1834) ; *that during that time hundreds of thousands of Africans were brought in; that the English absorbed these blacks; and that some of them became founders of titled families?*

Furthermore that since American whites are descended from English and other Euopean whites that some of the early American colonists were of this Negro ancestry, too.

Hundreds of pictures in the book clinch the facts. Given are over 200 pictures of Negroes in the coats-of-arms of these great European families, some of whom signify ancestry from Negroes. Many additional pictures from ancient Egypt down through the centuries to present-day Europe are given, including offspring of American Negro soldiers in World Wars I and II. Three chapters, with pictures, deal with race mixture in the United States.

Most of the hundreds of pictures given are rare. One of the Queen Charlotte Sophia, a German princess, consort of George III, shows her Negro strain even more than the one given in Sex and Race. Queen Charlotte was grandmother of Queen Victoria and ancestress of George VI.

Another picture shows descent of a cousin of George VI from the Negro favorite of Peter the Great of Russia through Pushkin.

Negroes who appear in the coats-of-arms of European cities, are also reproduced. Among them are Black Madonnas and one of St. Peter, founder of the Catholic Church, who is shown as jet-black, and is described as being a Negro.

IT CAN POSITIVELY BE SAID THAT NEVER BEFORE HAS SO MANY RARE FACTS, SO MANY RARE PICTURES ON THE BURIED AND THE PRESENT DAY HISTORY OF THE MIXING OF WHITES AND BLACKS, EVER BEEN PRESENTED.

AND BECAUSE OF THE INCREDULITY WITH WHICH MANY WILL RECEIVE THIS BOOK, SOURCES, INCLUDING THE PAGES OF THE BOOK, ARE GIVEN.

ALL IS TOLD IN SIMPLE LANGUAGE THAT EVERYONE CAN UNDERSTAND.

Please note that "NATURE KNOWS NO COLOR-LINE," comes at the right moment. The United Nations has just announced a History of Mankind, going back to 300,000 *B.C. on which* 1000 *of the world's leading historians are working. Care must be taken that the Negro isn't given the usual treatment in this history. "NATURE KNOWS NO COLOR-LINE" will make such oversight more difficult, therefore please support it.*

BOULANGER (G.-R.). H. C. *Esclaves à vendre. — Slaves for sale.*

White woman and black man put up for sale in Algiers market. Drawn from life by G. R. Boulanger and exhibited in the Paris Spring Salon of 1888. (See No. 63 in this book. Also "Africa's Gift to America," pp. 46-58.)

"Nature Knows No Color-Line" is nicely bound and is on paper that brings out the pictures clearly.

It got out by a regular publishing firm with its high overhead, it could not be sold at less than $10. But since the aim here is to give information rather than make profit the price is only

EXCERPTS FROM SOME OF THE THOUSANDS OF COMMENTS AND LETTERS ON THE WORK OF J. A. ROGERS

•

"SEX AND RACE"

Dr. W. E. B. DuBois: "No man living has revealed so many important facts about the Negro as Rogers."

In the Supreme Court of the United States, October Term, 1949, No. 25, in the printed Brief Amicus Curiae on Behalf of the Civil Rights Committee of the National Bar Association, which dealt with jim-crow seating on the dining cars and which ended in victory, his "Sex and Race" was cited as an authority that the color-line in America had no scientific foundation. More than a page of the brief was devoted to supporting quotations from "Sex and Race." (pp. 18-19.)

H. L. Mencken, world-famed author, and dean of American letters: Immensely entertaining and even more instructive. There is something new on almost every page, and you present it with the utmost effectiveness . . . a very competent job."

Carl Murphy, editor, Baltimore Afro-American: "As enthusiastic as a sixteen-year old is J. A. Rogers. . . . His Sex and Race, was so hot he had to print it himself. . . . Rogers is an authority on mixed families and backs it up with years of study in the libraries of Europe and America.

"I read Sex and Race several times a year, for, until he came along, I never knew that such world figures as Hannibal, Queen Nefertiti of Egypt, Gustavus IV of Sweden, Robert Browning (the poet), the wife of Garibaldi (the Italian pariot), and Disraeli (English Prime Minister) if they lived in America could be jim-crowed because of their colored ancestors.

"Nowhere else in contemporary literature is told the story of the Black Virgin Marys worshipped in many shrines in Europe.

"I'm waiting for Rogers' new book. . . . He has infected me with his enthusiasm."

A. M. Wendell Malliet, Amsterdam News, N. Y.: "Sex and Race by that well-known traveler, historian and authority on the black race and its history, J. A. Rogers, is one of those books that was bound to be written and published. He has written the greatest work of his long career. Sex and Race tells the gripping and almost unbelievable story of sex relations between the races of men throughout the ages.

"Of course, Sex and Race will probably suffer the fate resulting from a conspiracy of silence from the reviewers of the great white newspapers and periodicals. Its facts and testimony are too strong to be reviewed away or ignored, once the book gets reviewed at all. . . . Sex and Race blasts for all time the puerilities of thought that lead to the utterly false assumption about pure races. Rogers has shown that mankind is a mongrel breed at is best."

Rev. George S. Singleton, Editor, Christian Recorder, Philadelphia, Pa.: "I have read with avidity and profound interest your fascinating and scientific treatise, Sex and Race. . . . You have made civilization and culture debtor to yourself. I can all the more appreciate what you have done because some years ago I taught ar .hropology and Negro history."

Theodore Stanford, Philadelphia Tribune: "J. A. Rogers, historian, superb, has made an inestimable contribution to the expanding archives of the black man's history.

"From little-known sources, he has compiled a mountain of data which should work powerfully towards rendering any Caucasian American Negrophobe afraid to peer upwards into the branches of his family tree. . . . Rogers' essay illustrates upon what treacherous ground the foundations of the well-known boasts of racial purity and white supremacy are laid. . . .

"Rogers' work serves as a valuable tool in the creation of a genuine history of bio-racial relations in this hemisphere. It is a historical poem of many and subtle overtones. For through the shaded windows of this study of racial admixture, one may look out broadly and understandingly upon the whole complex panorama of the American race problem. . . .

"It is a substance upon which the Negro mind may feed in its search for the truth concerning its immediate historical origins. It is a meat into which the teeth of Negro youth may sink with satisfaction. . . ."

George S. Schuyler, Pittsburgh Courier: "J. A. Rogers has surpassed Bob Ripley. The latter's 'Believe It or Not' is pushed into the shade by the former's 'Sex and Race,' the second volume of which came from the press this week. Volume 1 of 'Sex and Race' was something to set the world on fire but Volume 2 makes Vesuvius seem like a glacier. There are more astonishing and little known facts packed between the two covers of this second volume than you can find in any book you ever heard about.

"There are hundreds of racy anecdotes here that remind one of Krafft-Ebing and Massucio. There are tales about the great and near-great in both so-called races, that might have been lifted out of 'My Life and Loves' by Frank Harris. There are inspiring accounts of the achievements of distinguished mixed bloods in the United States with fine photographs of many leading figures in colored America; past and present.

"Rogers has spared no pains in getting the facts and the pictures, and spared no expense in bringing out a book that is typographically above par. It ought to have a big sale and certainly deserves it.

"For thirty years J. A. Rogers has given prodigally of his time, money and energy to get the truth about miscegenation. He has ransacked the libraries of the Americas, Europe and North Africa to find the facts that many people would prefer to keep hidden. He has done more than any writer I know to smash the myth about race and race purity. He has entered where more timorous writers have feared to tread. He has received no scholarships or subsidies from the various white funds and foundations. He has financed all his research, travels and publishing. We are all tremendously indebted to him and he deserves our support in the way he would best like to have it—by buying Sex and Race."

Warren M. Banner, Opportunity Magazine: "Valuable data have been called from many documents throughout the world, including statutes, court records and other source materials. The author's wide travels and contacts plus his profuse reading, both in this country and abroad, have furnished him with materials which have never before been condensed for consumption by modern readers of the English language.

"Those who have observed and otherwise had immediate contacts with the facts presented know too well the farce which has been sold to the general public on the whole race question. The author gives to those who would otherwise be misled unknown facts in this whole area of human relationship.

"A grand job has been done by a scholar who has had devoted years to this subject. Others have continuously and purposely avoided it except in closed sessions. Thousands know many of the facts in this field, but few dare to add the pen.

"Everyone interested in mankind should read this work. It is timely. Many photographs have been included, which enhance a tome otherwise interesting and easy to read."

James W. Ivy in The Crisis: "Sex and Race is an irresistible blend of enjoyment and enlightenment, of provocativeness and brilliant writing, of curious fact and humorous insight. It is a saga of miscegenation throughout the ages, rich in its historical background, and fully documented. Rogers gives proof of every statement he puts down. . . . The author's erudition is truly amazing. Rogers seems to have read just about everything that has ever been written on the Negro in the major European tongues. . . . So far as I know, this is the first book of its kind in any language, and the facts which Rogers has dug up are truly amazing."

W. P. Dabney in the Cincinnati Union: "The book of books for all interested in the vast intermixture of races. . . . SEX AND RACE is king of its class! So interesting that once begun, when the reading is done, the mind marvels over the countless wonders it contains. . . . The pictorial illustrations alone are invaluable. . . . Only $3.75 a copy, worth one hundred times as much."

Richard E. Mohr: "Backing his contentions by historical and scientific authority, the author has turned out a saga of miscegenation. Rich in historical background, the volume presents an exhaustive history, replete with almost countless wonders." The Butler Collegian.

Irene West, Los Angeles, Calif.: "Yours is the greatest cure yet that I have seen advanced to knock the wind out of the 'white supremacy' sails. To dig up their ancestry (drag the skeletons out of the closets) would rock the foundations of the South and scare all the other States half to death."

Ezra D. Anderson, Jr., student: "Your Sex and Race has been acclaimed by many white students here at the University of Minnesota as one of the most brilliantly written volumes of our times.

"Some admitted that reading your three volumes has caused them to respect the many obstacles and prejudices formulated against the Negro. It was their first time to read about the Negro from first hand research."

The Voyage of the Sable Venus from Angola, West Africa, to the West Indies, escorted by a White Neptune and a nimbus of white Cupids. Painted by T. Stothard in 1818. Fanciers of fair black femininity from Boston, Mass., to Buenos Aires used to await the slave-ships for the arrival of these black Venuses.

(See "Poetic Expressions on the Black Woman by White Western Writers" in "Sex and Race," Vol. II, pp. 217-220, (1942).

Georgia Douglas Johnson: "We are still reading your astounding books. Sex and Race is in the Library of Congress section of RARE BOOKS. . . .

"You are unique. No one else has attempted what you so powerfully performed."

Raymond Combs, USMM: "May I congratulate you heartily and sincerely on your Sex and Race. I am not alone in this opinion. It is the same as hundreds of others of our fighting men that I know have read them."

ON WORLD'S GREAT MEN OF COLOR

George S. Schuyler: "We owe a double debt to J. A. Rogers for the immense research which enabled him to write his 'World's Great Men of Color: 3000 B.C. to 1946 A.D.' Never again will there be any excuse for anybody anywhere to remain ignorant of the Negro genius in all lands and its immense contribution to world culture. Between two covers now lies the fruits of decades of research in the greatest libraries and museums of the world. Whether you are reading about Imhotep, Egyptian god of medicine, or St. Maurice of Aganum, patron saint of Germany, or Paul DuChadllu, you will feel indebted to J. A. Rogers for his grand contribution to learning and better understanding."

Louis A. Potter: "As a teacher in the Philadelphia schools I realize fully how great a need your contribution will fill. Not only in Philadelphia but throughout America and the world in general we suffer from an abyssmal lack of inspirational knowledge of our own. You bridge that gap in a grand manner.

"May I commend you for the effortless style that enables one to fairly flow through the book, making it possible thereby to devote one's entire attention to the absorption of the mass of material without the necessity of constant interpretation.

"Wishing you great success in your tremendous effort. . . . May it be the dawn of an ever increasing wave of knowledge that must necessarily cause every Negro to hold his head a bit higher and all others who read your book to view the Negro with a loftier perspective."

Rose Wilder Lane, noted author, "Who's Who in America," says of "World's Great Men of Color": An omnivorous reader such as I am, has a habit of classifying books. Dismissing the quantities of trash of all categories, three remain the entertaining books, the currently informative books, some books of more permanent worth, a few indispensable ones, and rarely a new one that tentatively may be called great.

"Now here is a book of such magnitude that it overlaps all these categories and goes into none. For three months I have been reading it with unflagging interest, with delight, amusement, excitement, profit admiration and increasing dismay, for I must tell you about this book and I don't think I can.

"I have thought of comparing it to Plutarch's Lives but then it more nearly resembles the History of the Father of History; yet it is American and contemporary, too. . . .

"The author of the book is as difficult to classify as his work. Mr. J. A. Rogers is an American and a self-made scholar. He is an historian of enormous erudition. He is an anthropologist of no small caliber, elected in 1930 to membership in the Paris Society of Anthropology. He has lectured at the Sorbonne and other leading European universities. He is a linguist, a world traveller, a journalist, an author, and, I would judge from references in his writings, a connoisseur of antique art.

This book is a product of more than thirty years research in the world's libraries and museums, and of experience in many countries. . . .

"I know no easier, more fascinating way to begin to acquire the world-view, innocent of propaganda or bias, based on fact, which no American learns from schools or the daily press, than reading World's Great Men of Color." From the Economic Council Review of Books, June 1947.

"FROM SUPERMAN TO MAN"

DR. HUBERT HARRISON, lecturer for the Board of Education, New York City: "A genuine treasure. I still insist that From 'Superman' to Man is the greatest book ever written in English on the Negro and I am glad to know that increasing thousands of black and white readers re-echo the high opinion of it which I had expressed some years ago."

DR. W. E. B. DUBOIS: *The person who wants in small compass in good English and in attractive form the arguments for the present Negro position should buy and read and recommend to his friends "From Superman to Man."*

GEORGE S. SCHUYLER: The array of facts and the incomparable logic is astounding. It seems almost impossible that so much information has been squeezed into 128 pages. Rogers is undoubtedly the most widely read and informed person on the relation between the races, white or black, in the United States today. * * * The research of a score of years is placed at the disposal of a racial group sadly in need of such ammunition in the keen and ever-present struggle for their full rights and opportunities as American citizens.

GEORGE W. ELLIS, F.R.G.S. (for eight years Secretary of the United States Legation to Liberia): *"Its breadth of scholastic research, its selection and concentration of matter are as amazing as its wealth of information. The book is well written and the skilful management of materials shows not only the author's mastery of the subject, but his knowledge of the technique of the literary art. In the program of the broadest education of the races and the promotion of social accord and co-operation this volume should be in every library and home of the country. In his absorbing story we see the souls of the white and darker groups groping and struggling toward a better day of peace and good understanding between the races."*

NEGRO YEAR BOOK, Tuskegee Institute: *"From Superman to Man is a valuable addition to the literature of the race and should be widely read."*

WHAT SOME LEADING WHITE PEOPLE HAVE SAID

MISS Z. BABER, Instructor, University of Chicago: *"From Superman to Man is the best literature I have read on the subject. I am placing it on the required reading list for my classes."*

THE BROOKLYN EAGLE: "From Superman to Man is a vindication of the American Negro."

DR. W. N. C. CARLTON, Librarian, Newberry Library, Chicago, Ill. (in a letter to the author): *"I shall place your book in the permanent collection of the Library where present and future students of the history of the Negro race will find it a most significant document."*

N. Y. EVENING POST: "This porter who attended Yale had travelled extensively and spoke several languages, had at his fingers' ends the arguments necessary to prove that his race was not a whit inferior to the Caucasian."

MISS MARY WHITE OVINGTON, Chairman, Board of Directors, N. A. C. P.: *"Anyone who wants to be provided with an enormous stock of information confuting the doctrine of white courtesy debating the race question with a rabid Southern Senator."*

THE BOSTON TRANSCRIPT: "If this book could be placed in the hands of every creator of public opinion in the United States it might bring about a revolution in the country's attitude toward the Negro. * * * The argument for the rights and better treatment of the Negro and for the essential equality of the different so-called races is indisputable. * * * The author's breadth of research, store of information, fascinating style and convincing logic are notable. This is the fourth edition and doubtless many other editions will follow."

THE CATHOLIC BOARD FOR MISSION WORK AMONG THE COLORED PEOPLE, New York City: *"We have read with much interest and pleasure your book, From Superman to Man. There are more objections against the colored race answered in this book more satisfactorily and convincingly than in any book we have read upon the question. We intend using it as a text-book for our own advancement in the knowledge of the race question. Please send us 25 copies at once."*

SEX AND RACE

History of the Mixing of White and Black from Prehistoric Times to the Present.

Read what happens to white Anglo-Saxon superiority and Nazi super-superiority when they meet the sex lure of the Black Race.

New York Times, July 1, 1940 (early edition, p. 19) says: "NEGROID BLOOD IN HITLER ARYANS." Which is not surprising. Europe is only eleven miles away from Africa.

AN AMAZING BOOK FOR AMAZING TIMES

Written by J. A. Rogers, author "From Superman to Man," etc., after a life-time of travel in many foreign lands and searching through tens of thousands of rare and ancient documents; as well as his own observations.

VOLUME ONE—THE MIXING OF BLACK AND WHITE IN THE OLD WORLD

Some of the features are:

This Mongrel World. Mixing of white and black in the United States more truly American than Plymouth Rock. The Spaniard and the Negro lived in the United States 107 years before the coming of the Pilgrim Fathers.

The first men were Negritos, or little Negroes. Mixing of Black and White in Europe about 50,000 B.C. A Mulatto Race of 30,000 B.C. How the White Race originated.

Mixing of black and white in Ancient Egypt, Greece, Rome. Black, mulatto, and white rulers of Egypt intermarry freely.

Mixing of black and white in India, China, Japan, Australia, Hawaii. The first Chinese were Negroes.

Origin of the Jews. Moses and leading Biblical characters, Negroes. The Jews today.

BLACK GODS AND MESSIAHS. Showing the Negro origin of civilization in the ancient Old and New World. The rise of the Mulattoes. The Rise of the Whites.

Mixing of White and Black in Africa, with special treatment of Ethiopia, Morocco, and South Africa. Spain, Portugal, Austria, Russia, Germany, Holland, the British Isles.

Individual Romances. True love story of a German woman and a Senegalese soldier. THE BLACK NUN, daughter of Maria Theresa, Queen of France and a Negro, who was a prisoner for life because of her color. ISABEAU, Haitian charmer who won the heart of a French king.

PAULINE BONAPARTE, Napoleon's sister and her Negro lovers in Haiti and France. THE BLACK VENUS—Jeanne Duval, a Haitian girl, who won the heart of Baudelaire, France's greatest poet, and inspired his verse. Count Munck, Negro father of Gustavus IV of Sweden.

SCANDALS OF RACE-MIXING IN ENGLAND, one of which concerns a cousin of George V, and was aired in the London courts in 1932.

Profusely illustrated with pictures ancient and modern. SEX AND RACE takes you into an atmosphere of higher thought. You'll meet here the leading scientists in their respective fields. Quotations from the great anthropologists, archaeologists, Egyptologists, historians, philosophers of all ages—Aristotle, Plutarch, Tacitus, Quintilian, Jornandes, St. Jerome, Azurara, Masuccio, Shakespeare, Von Luschan, Finot, Petrie, Breasted, Anatole France, Baudelaire, Romain Rolland, Einstein—and many others—all strung together with the author's own thirty years' of research and travel in fifty lands.

Everything—no matter how sensational it may sound—is backed up by the leading historical and scientific authority. Footnotes throughout the book, giving authors and pages. You will get acquainted with a great number of books you probably never heard of before.

VOLUME TWO—MIXING OF WHITE AND BLACK IN THE NEW WORLD

Black and white in America before Columbus. Race-Mixing in all the South and Central American Lands and the West Indies from the 16th Century.

THE UNITED STATES. The Negro first arrived in 1513, not 1619. Race-Mixing in the different states with case-histories by well-known writers.

History of the Mixing of the White Man and the Black Woman in the United States.

History of the Mixing of the Black Man and the White Woman in the United States.

Which attracts the other more strongly, White or Black?

Which is Sexually Superior, white or black? Opinions of the world's leading sexologists.

Race attraction among Nordic homosexuals, men and women, in America, England, and Germany.

Black concubines of American presidents, and leading Americans with Negro blood.

Is the Mulatto superior in intellect and initiative to the unmixed Negro as many scientists claim?

SEX AND RACE, Volume Three—WHY WHITE AND BLACK MIX IN SPITE OF ALL LAWS AND SOCIAL POSITION. Race mixture discussed in its religious, scientific, and sentimental phases. Brings you up-to-date on what history and science have said on race mixture from the days of the Greeks and Romans to our times. The most ticklish phases of the race question frankly discussed. A veritable encyclopedia of rare facts, ancient and modern. Bibliography of scientific books, novels and plays on the race question and books that oppose racialism and others that favor it. 27 pages of index for the three volumes of Sex and Race. Hundreds of portraits.

H. L. Mencken, dean of American letters, in a letter to the author, says of Sex and Race, "You are immensely entertaining and even more instructive. There is something new on almost every page, and you present it with the utmost effectiveness. My congratulations on a very competent job."

"AFRICA'S GIFT TO AMERICA"

THE AFRICAN-AMERICAN IN THE MAKING AND SAVING OF THE UNITED STATES

AMAZING REVELATIONS IN THE STORY OF THE NEGRO IN AMERICA! THE TRUTH AT LAST!

Did you know that Africa and its people brought to the New World did most in the early building of the United States?

A white Texas judge praising his black mammy said recently, "The first nutrition I ever received came from the bosom of a Negro woman." The same is true of America's first economic nutrition. It came from the bosom of Africa.

Did you know that without the Negro's help the American Revolution could not have been won? Also the war of 1812?

That Abraham Lincoln said five times the Negro was the decisive force that won the Civil War? He said he used them because "I felt we had reached the end of our rope; that we had about played the last card."

That Negroes owned white slaves in America? These and many other facts are given with proof and hundreds of pictures.

HERE IS WHAT'S BEING SAID OF "AFRICA'S GIFT TO AMERICA":

B. M. Kibasa, Tabora, of Tanganyika Government, East Africa: "I must state emphatically that the book is a tremendous work and so much is in it that in fact it should have been sold at a higher price. So far I have read it four times. I read and re-read just to cram my head with the indisputable facts. I had never known that the Black Man had contributed so much to the salvation of the United States. . . ."

Dr. Horace Mann Bond, Dean of the School of Education, Atlanta University: "Your Africa's Gift to America . . . is a work of inestimable value. . . . Congratulations. Appreciation. Gratitude. . . ."

Dr. E. C. Mazique, President National Medical Assn.: "I am simply overwhelmed by the wonderful contribution that you have made to Negro history and the potential you still have in shaping the future course of America. . . ."

Elijah Muhammad, "You have contributed to our people the most valuable knowledge of their history under the slavemaster than any other writer. . . . Your name and work shall ever be remembered in the nation of the black man. . . ."

Booker T. Alexander, Imperial Potentate, Nobles of the Mystic Shrine: "Every Afro-American youngster from the age of twelve years should be required to read this very important book as well as every Afro-American adult. Very, very few public schools teach our youth the facts of American history as it relates to our ancestors. The fathers, mothers, and adult relatives must assume this responsibility. . . ."

James W. Ivy, in Crisis Magazine: "This is an excellent book. Mr. Rogers has taken in significant facts, digested them, and he now presents them in an immensely readable study. The book is lavishly illustrated."

ALSO BY J. A. ROGERS

Africa's Gift to America		$24.95
Sex & Race	Vol. 1, the old world	$19.95
	Vol. 2, the new world	$19.95
	Vol. 3, why white & black...	$19.95
From Superman to Man		$15.00
Nature Knows No Color Line		$15.00
As Nature Leads		$15.00
The Real Facts About Ethiopia		$6.95
100 Amazing Facts About the Negro		$6.95
Five Negro Presidents		$5.95

The Afro-American July 24, 1954

Haile's gold medal awarded to Rogers

NEW YORK — By imperial command of Emperor, Haile Selassie, J. A. Rogers was summoned to the Waldorf-Astoria last Thursday, presented with a gold medal and given an order for 128 copies of Rogers' book, "World's Great Men of Color, 3000 B.C. to 1946 A.D."

After the presentation, Mr. Rogers said:

"This ought to squelch the belief held by some that he considers himself white and is not interested in colored Americans.

"I first met him at his coronation in 1930.

"At 61, the Emperor is in excellent health. He underwent a physical examination at Harknes Pavilion of the Presbyterian Hospital and passed with flying colors."

Mr. Rogers revealed he is working on two new books.

One of them is a book of amazing facts entitled "Astonishing Facts About the Colored American, 1512 to the Present."

Mr. Rogers says he has enough important facts to fill several volumes.

Wording In Amharic

The gold coin, given him by the Emperor, is one of a thousand minted for the Emperor's coronation and the wordings in Amharic.

Commenting on John Gunther's story in the Reader's Digest in which said Gunther the Ethiopians "consider themselves to be white no matter what their color is," this is an entirely false interpretation.

"Ethiopians do consider themselves the equal of anybody, which is something entirely different," says Mr. Rogers.

Only In U.S.

"I discussed this with many of the highest Ethiopians. They regard themselves as black people — Africans.

Rogers Guest of Selassie

NEW YORK — Emperor Haile Selassie of Ethiopia sent for and granted private audience to J. A. Rogers, Courier editorial page columnist, on the day of his departure.

The Emperor met Mr. Rogers in Ethiopia in 1930 at his coronation and again in 1935 when Mr. Rogers was in Addis Ababa as a Courier correspondent.

CHARLOTTE SOPHIA
Queen of England
consort of George III,
great-great-grandmother of George VI
(see Notes on the Illustrations in SEX and RACE.)

Facsimile from

THE NEW YORK TIMES

MONDAY, JULY 1, 1940.

NEGROID BLOOD IN HITLER'S 'ARYANS'

Ancestries Traced in Book on Racial Mixture Published in Berlin

MANY PEOPLES SHOW IT

Strain of Negro Is Shown in Circles of Russian, English and German Nobility

On the thesis that no national entity can correctly designate itself as a race and that the people of these entities have in their veins more Negroid blood than is generally supposed, Brunold Springer, in his "Racial Mixture as a Basic Principle of Life," just published by Verlag der Neuen Generation of Berlin, analyzes from the Negroid point of view the characteristics of the so-called "Hitler Aryan," who Der Fuehrer would have prevail in Germany. He writes:

Ofter the Negroid aspect is strikingly evidenced in personal appearance, Herr Springer writes, as in the case of Dr. Schweninger, Bismarck's physician, who had warm, African eyes, or of Beethoven, who possessed in addition a strain of Malay or Alpine blood as well. Once the characteristic Negro features become familiar to the glance, blonde Negroes are often discernible. Gabrielle Réjane, the French actress, had the broad nose and heavy lips of the blond Negroid type.

Black Strain in Spaniards

There is a very large percentage of Negro blood in the Spanish people. . . . The Spaniards then carried the black strain farther into Europe, into France and the former Netherlands. When the Spaniards were driven out of the latter lands, about 3,000 of them settled in Hamburg, and many a Hamburg citizen today bears a striking resemblance to the citizens of Spain.

Portugal was the first example of a Negrito republic in Europe. In the Portuguese runs a deep current of Negro blood, and there the Negro has often risen to the caste of the nobility. . . . All of this is ancient history. The Romans brought Negro troops to the Rhine and over the Donau. Later merchants purchased the young Negroes as servants; in all large cities of commerce there were several hundred blacks, and many a house was known simply as "at the Moors."

In one circle of people whose members belong to the Russian, English and German nobility there is much Negro blood, inherited from an ancestor who lived at the end of the eighteenth century, and who was the great-grandfather of one of the greatest poets of all lands and of all times, Alexander Sergeivitch Pushkin.

(For hundreds of pictures of these European families with Negro ancestors see: NATURE KNOWS NO COLOR-LINE).